Country Farm Coloring Book For Adults

Relax and breathe the kind air of the countryside thanks to these 52 drawing to be colored, for adults. You'll find animals, tractors, landscapes, fruit and much more.

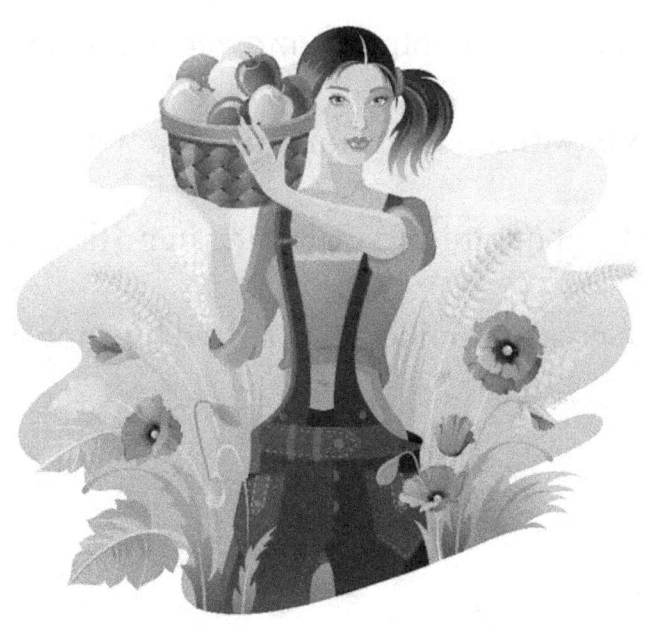

If you liked this book it would be great if you leave an honest review on the site from which you purchased this book.

Copyright 2019

All right reserved.

No part of this publication may be reproduced, distributed or transmitted in any form or any means including photocopying, recording or other electronic or mechanical methods, without the prior written permission of the publisher except in the case of brief quotations embodied in critical reviews and certyain other non commercial uses permitted by copyright law.

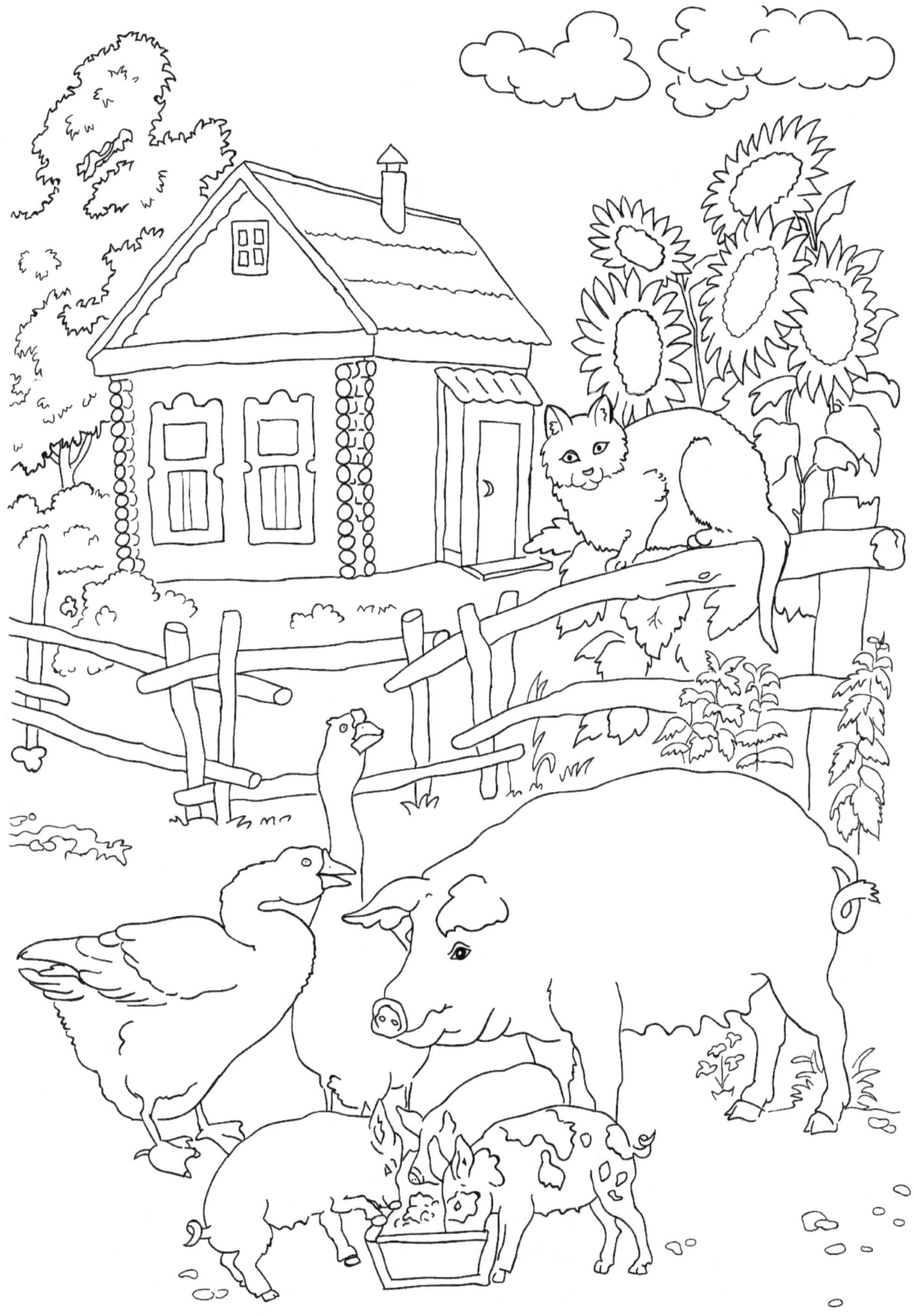

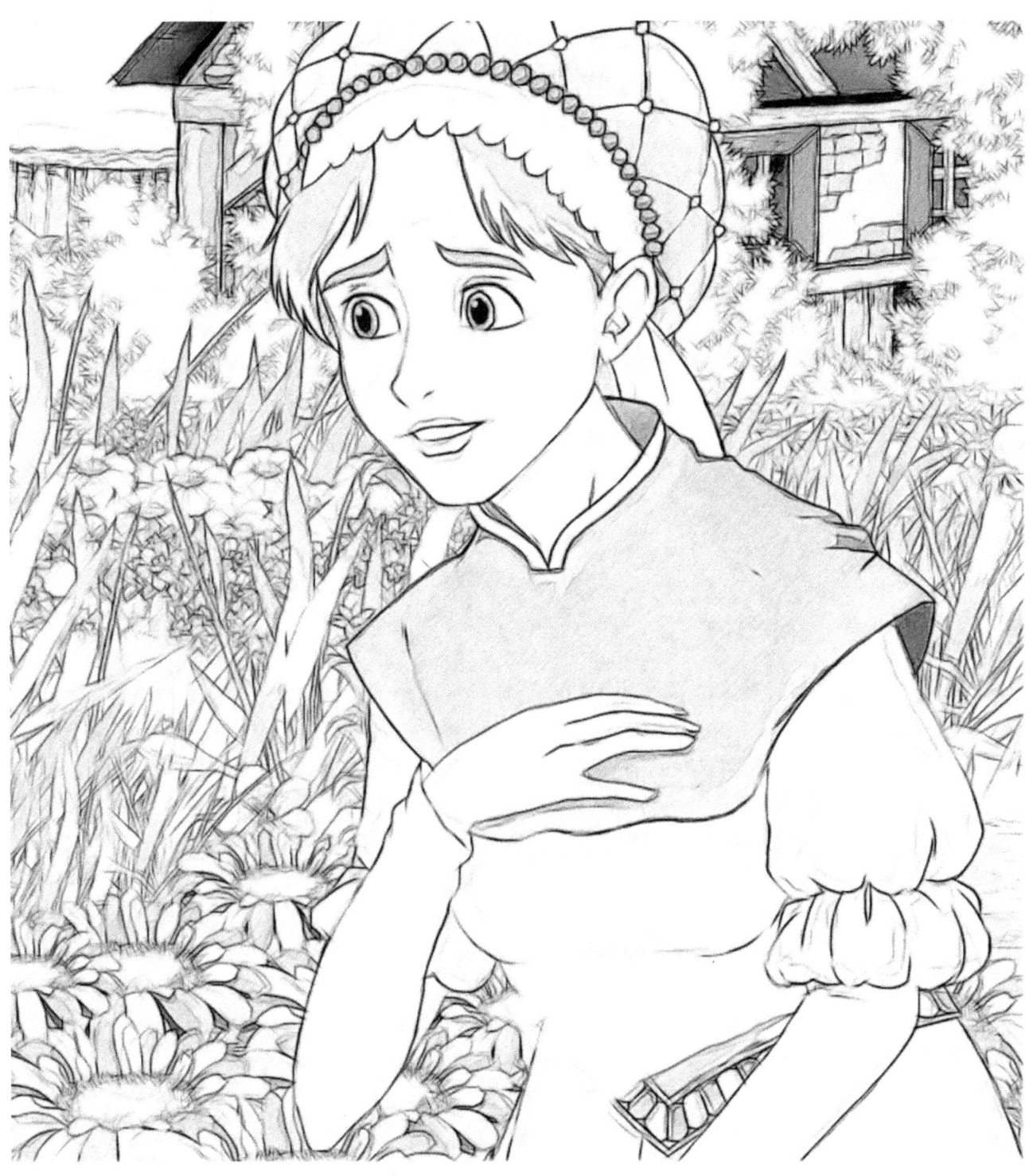

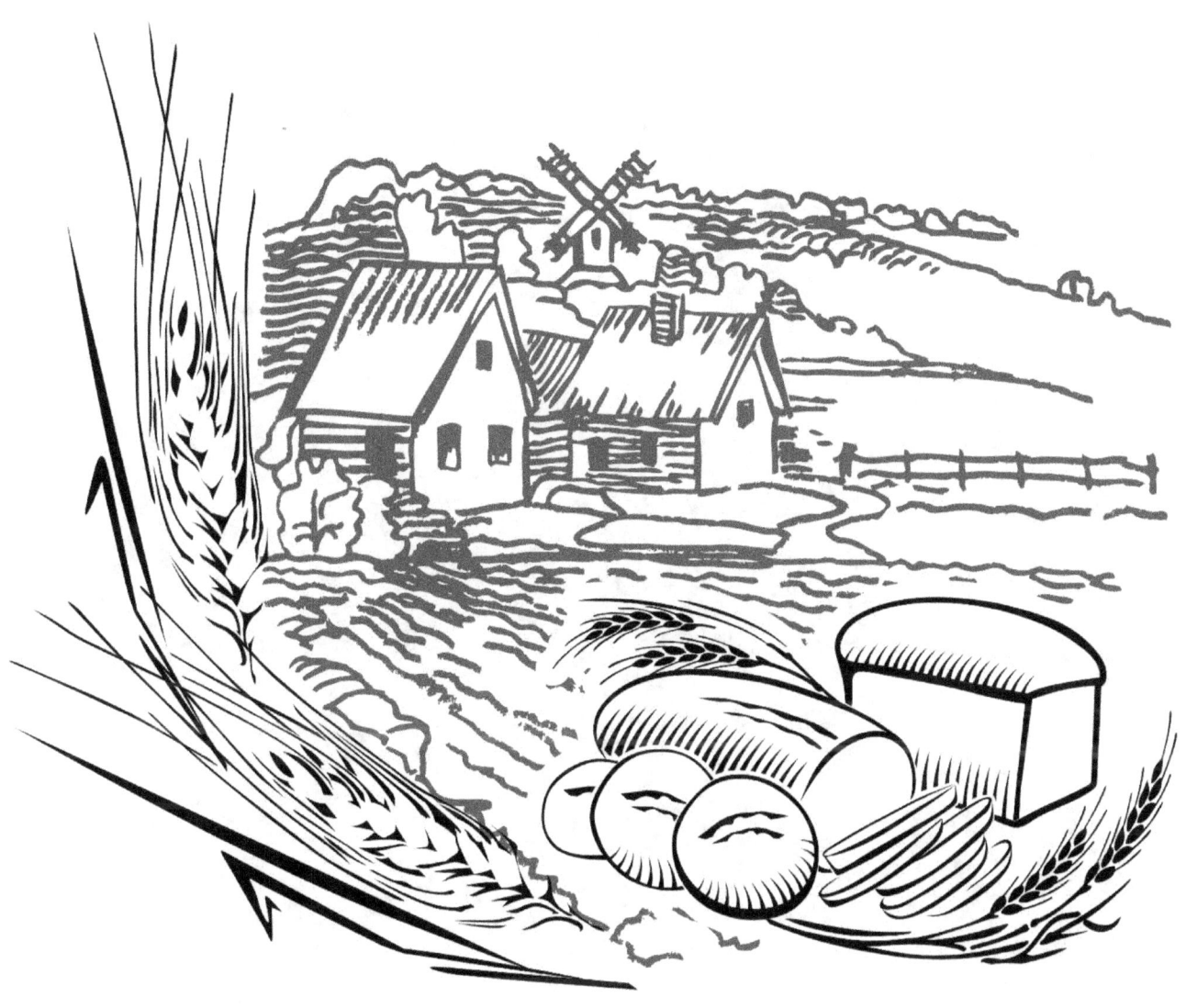

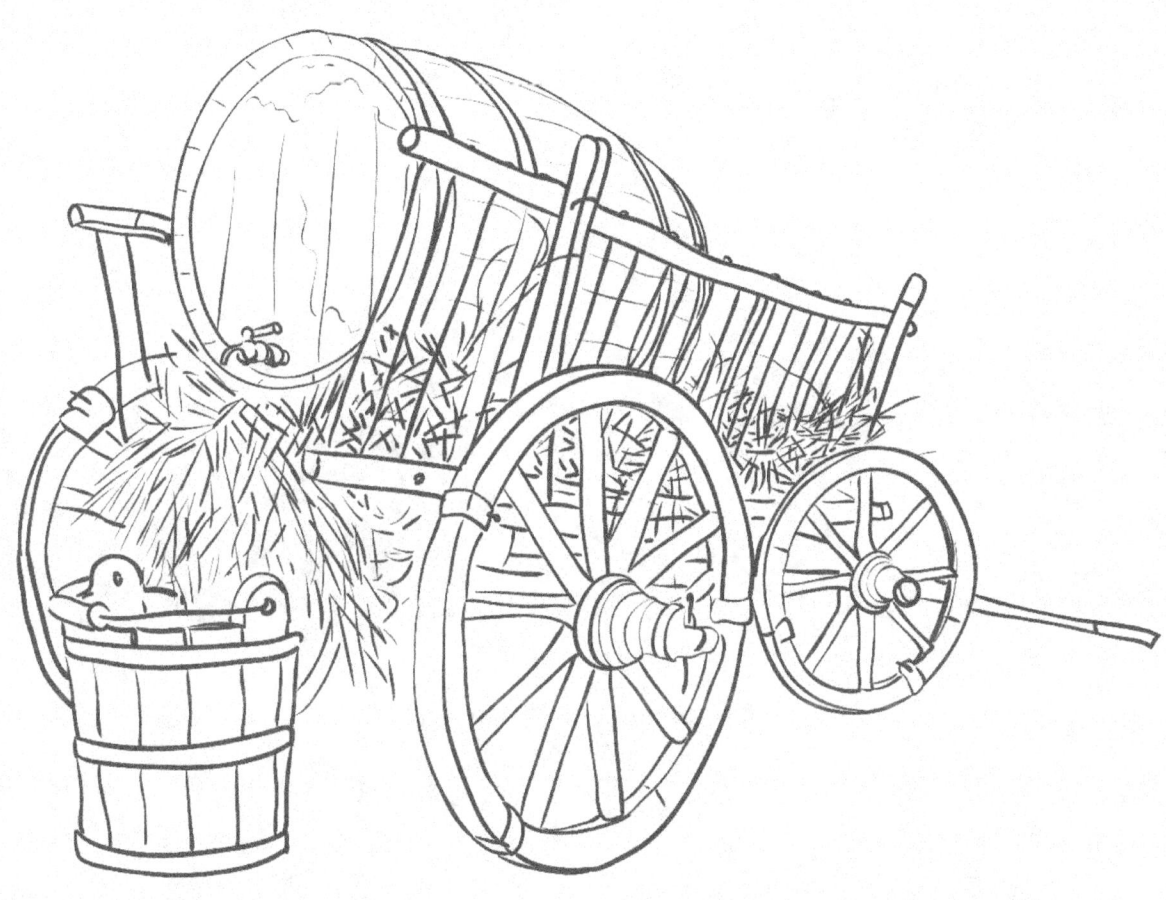

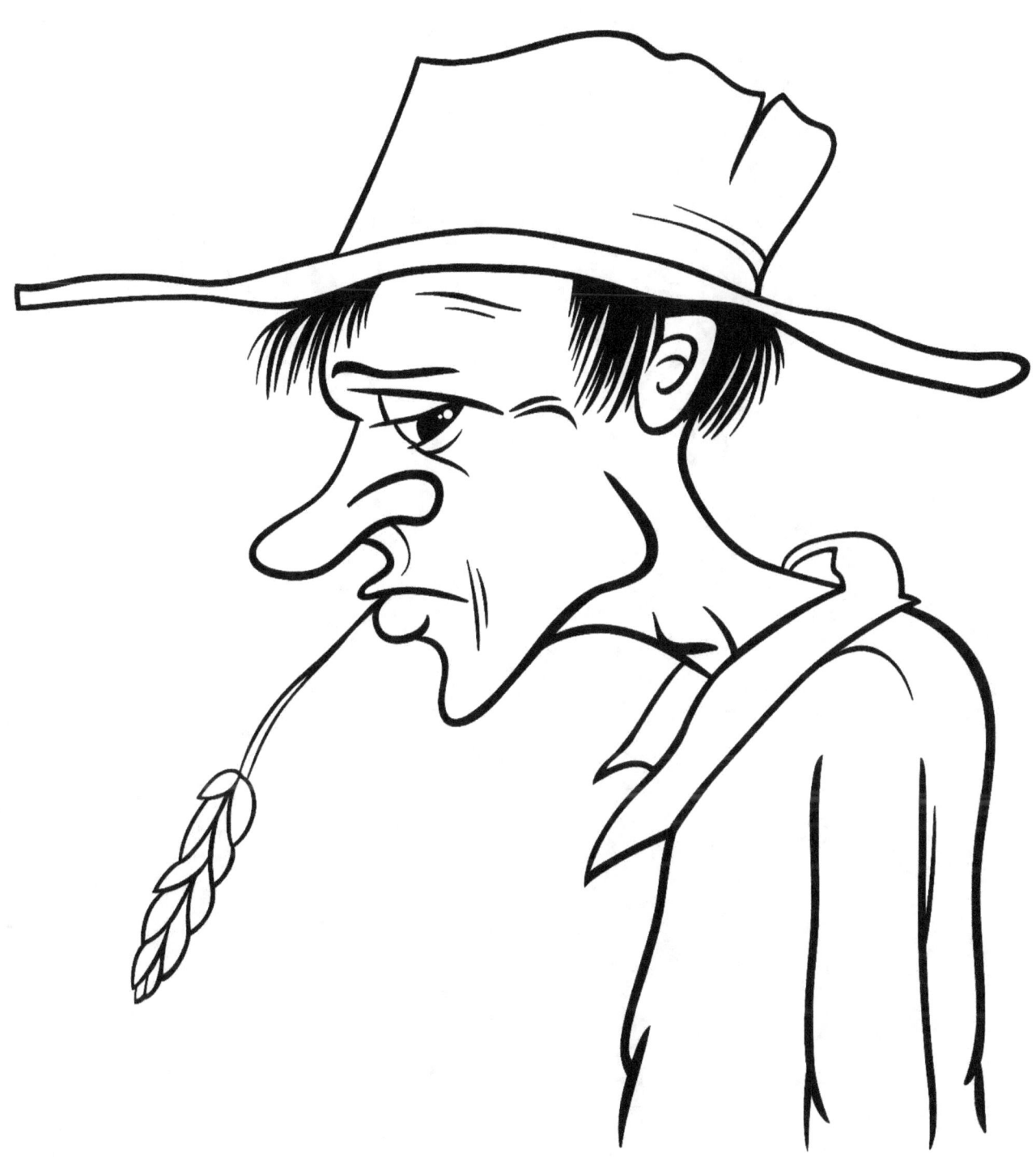

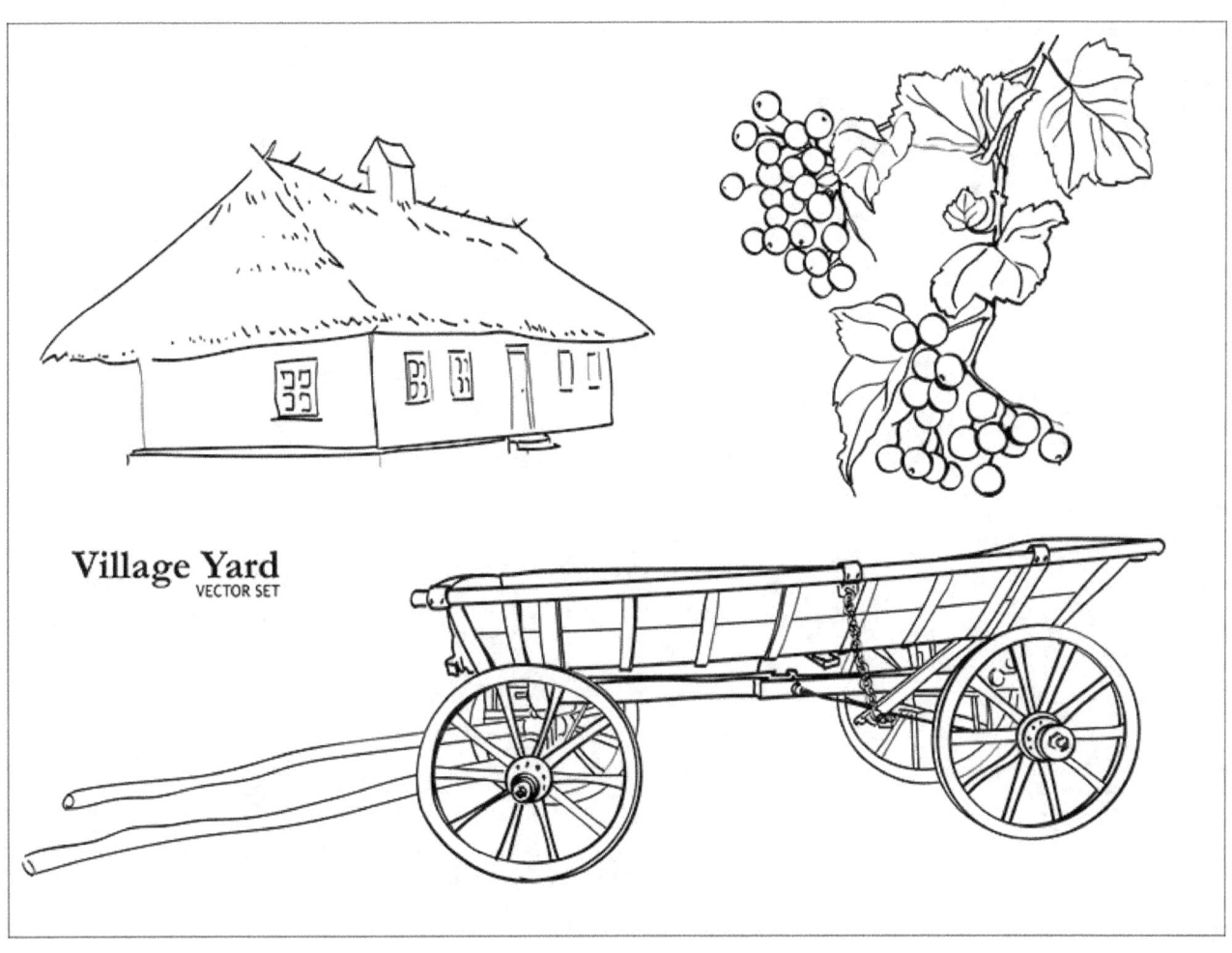

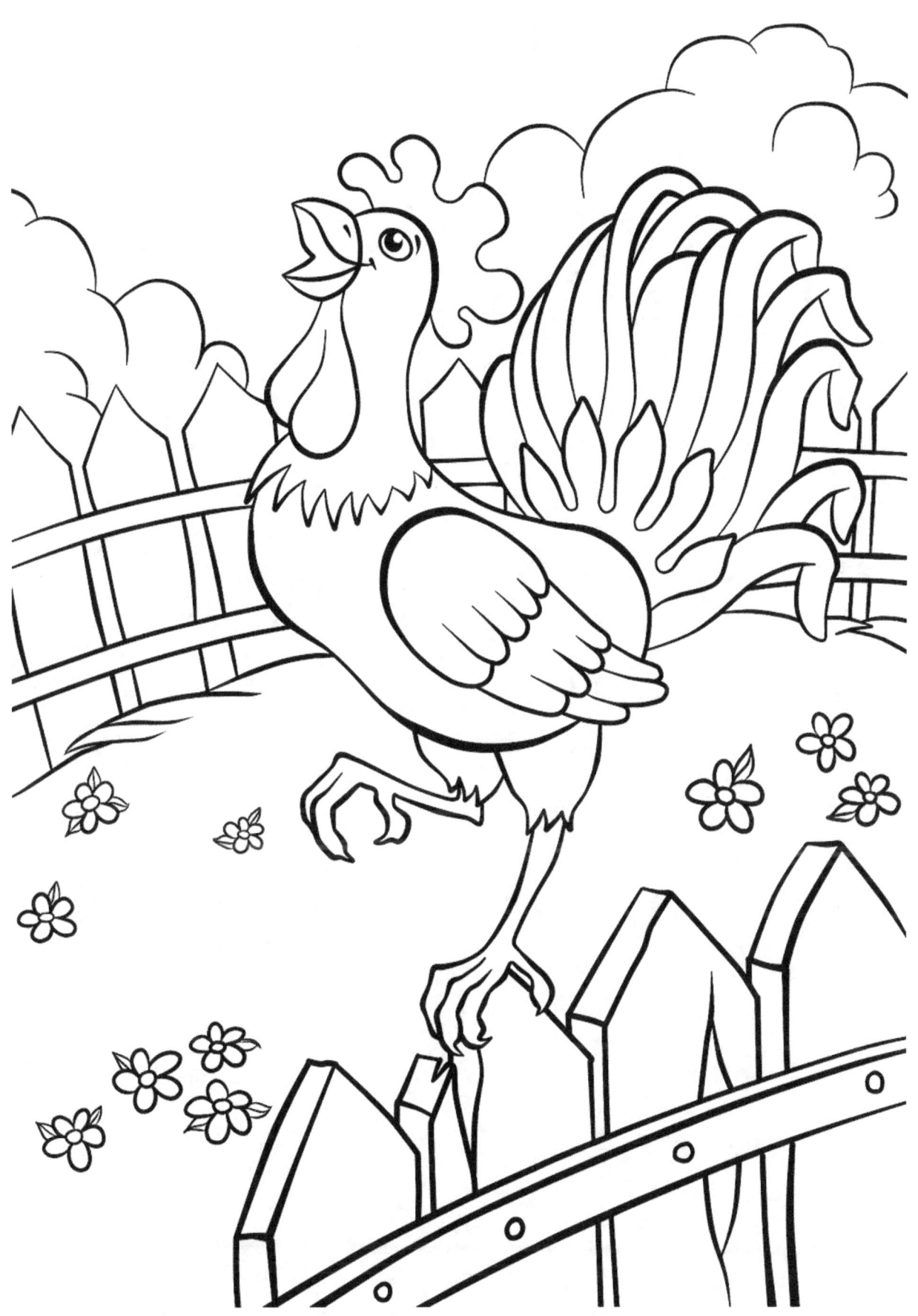

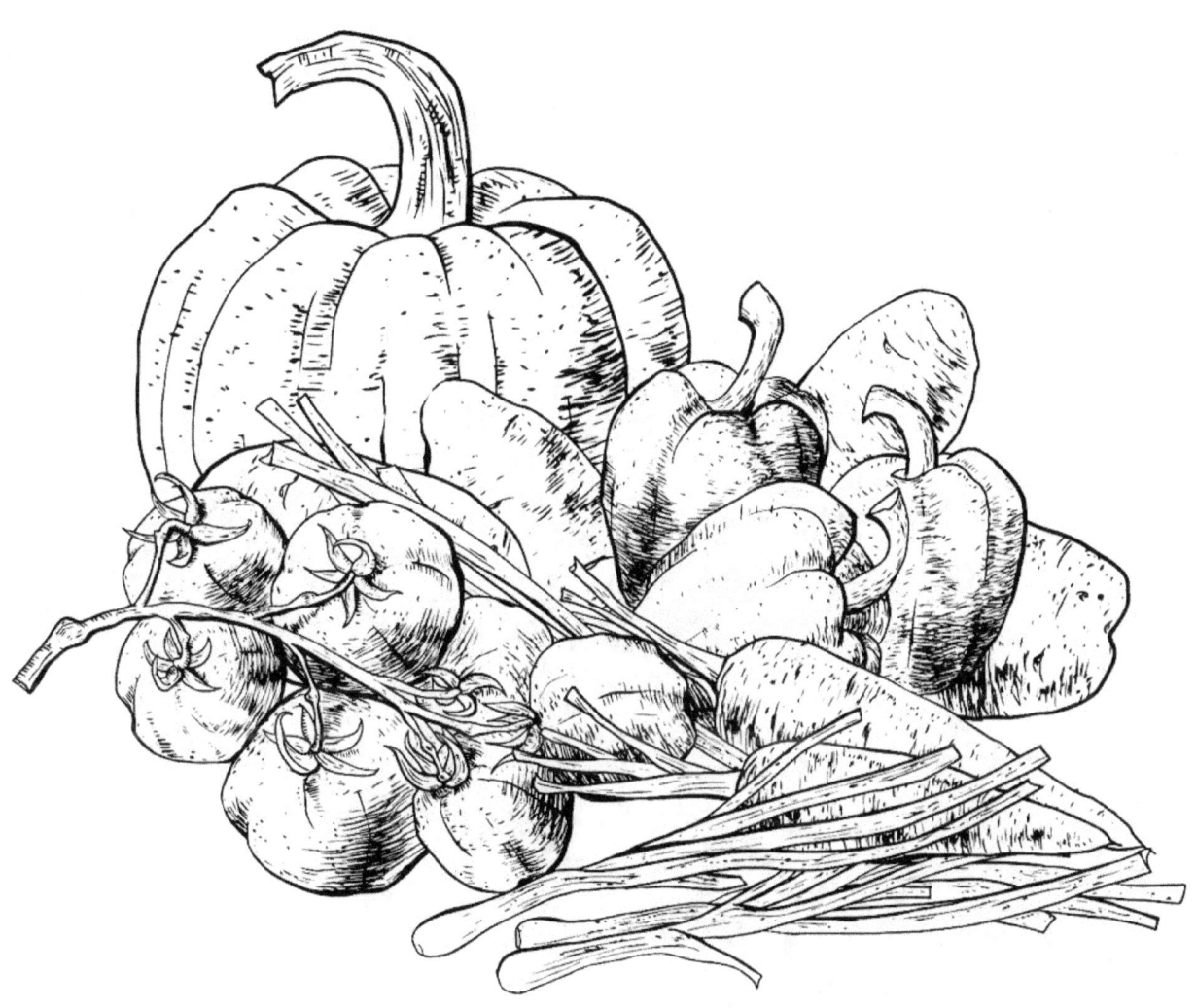

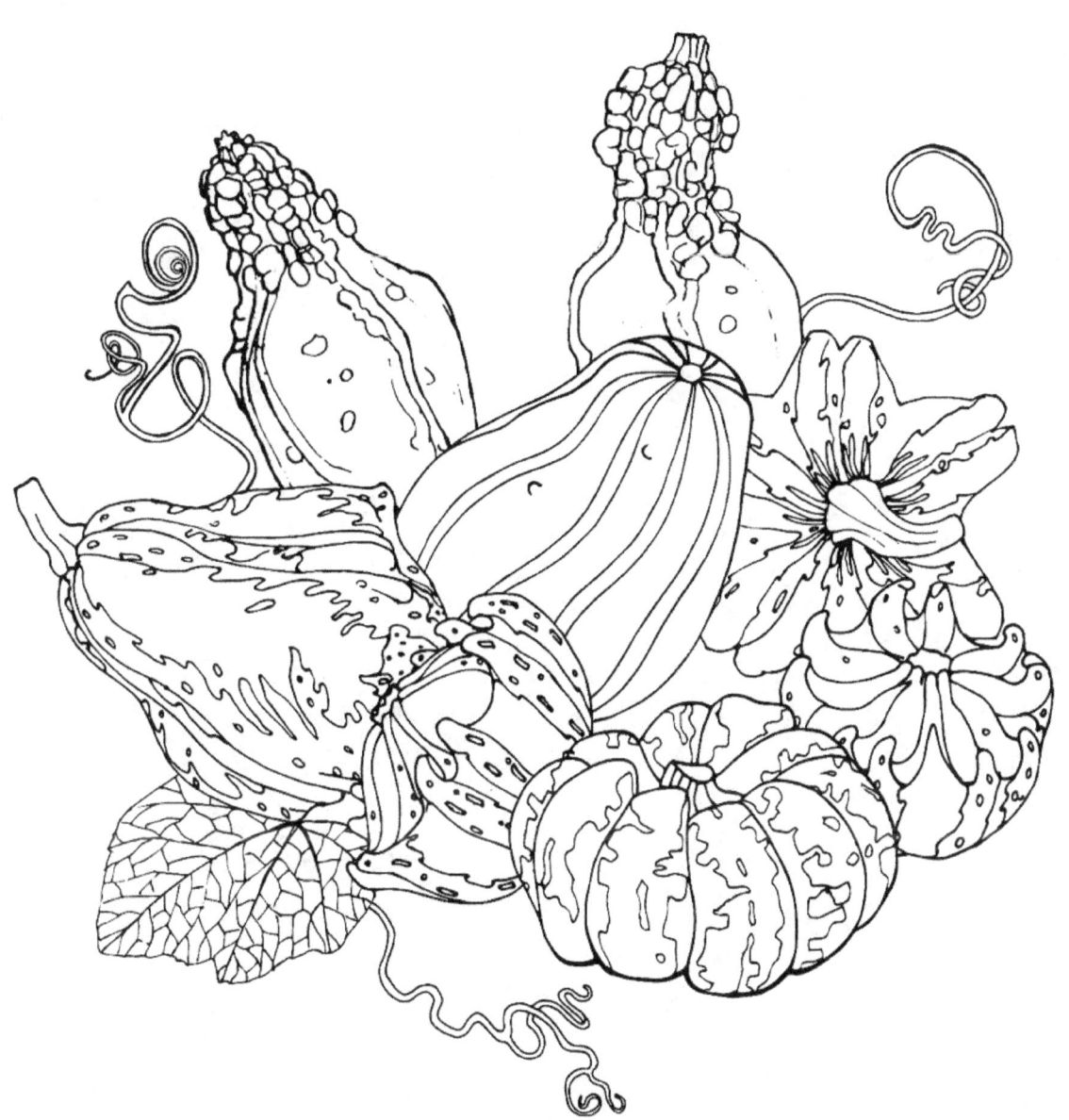

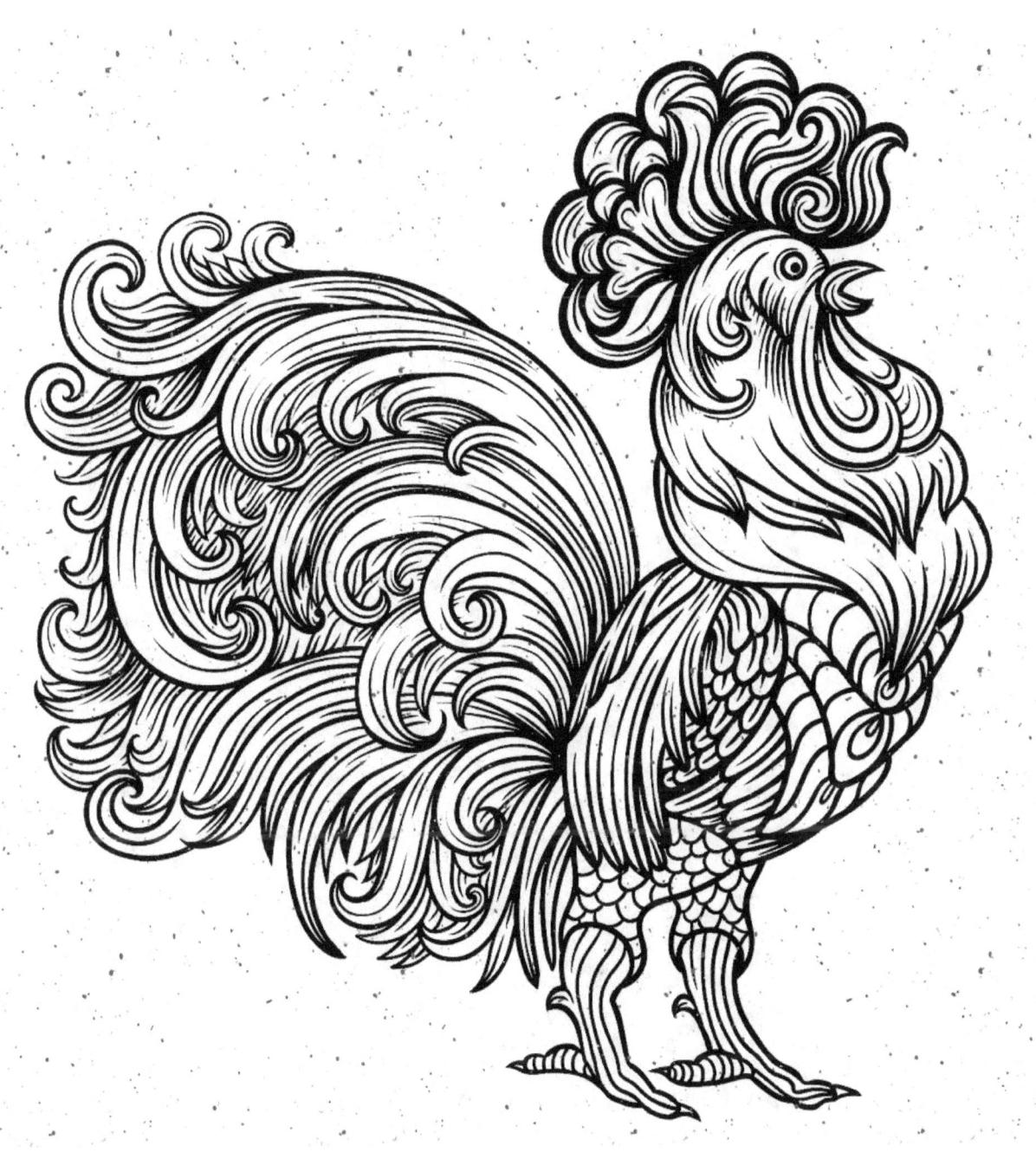

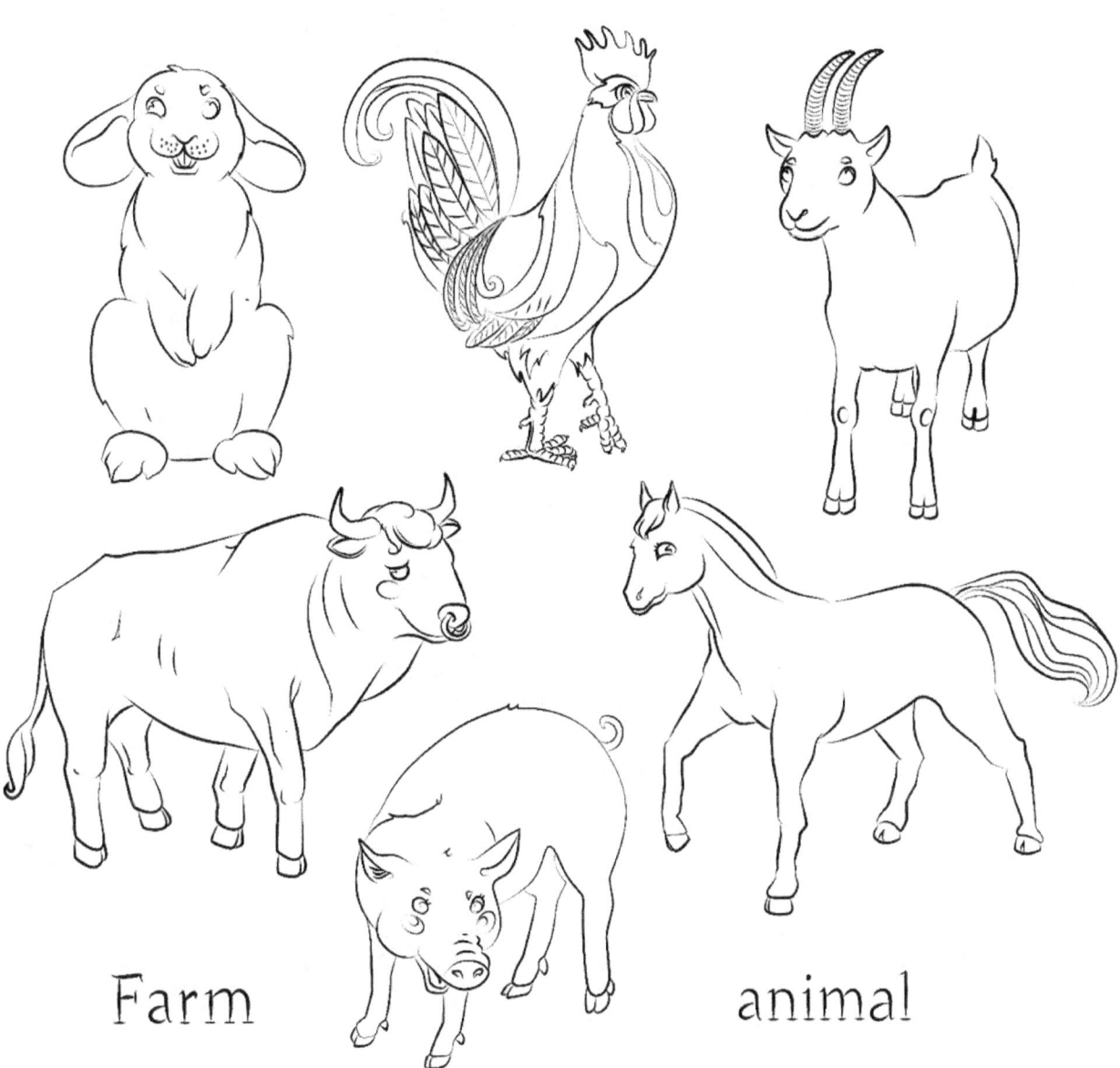

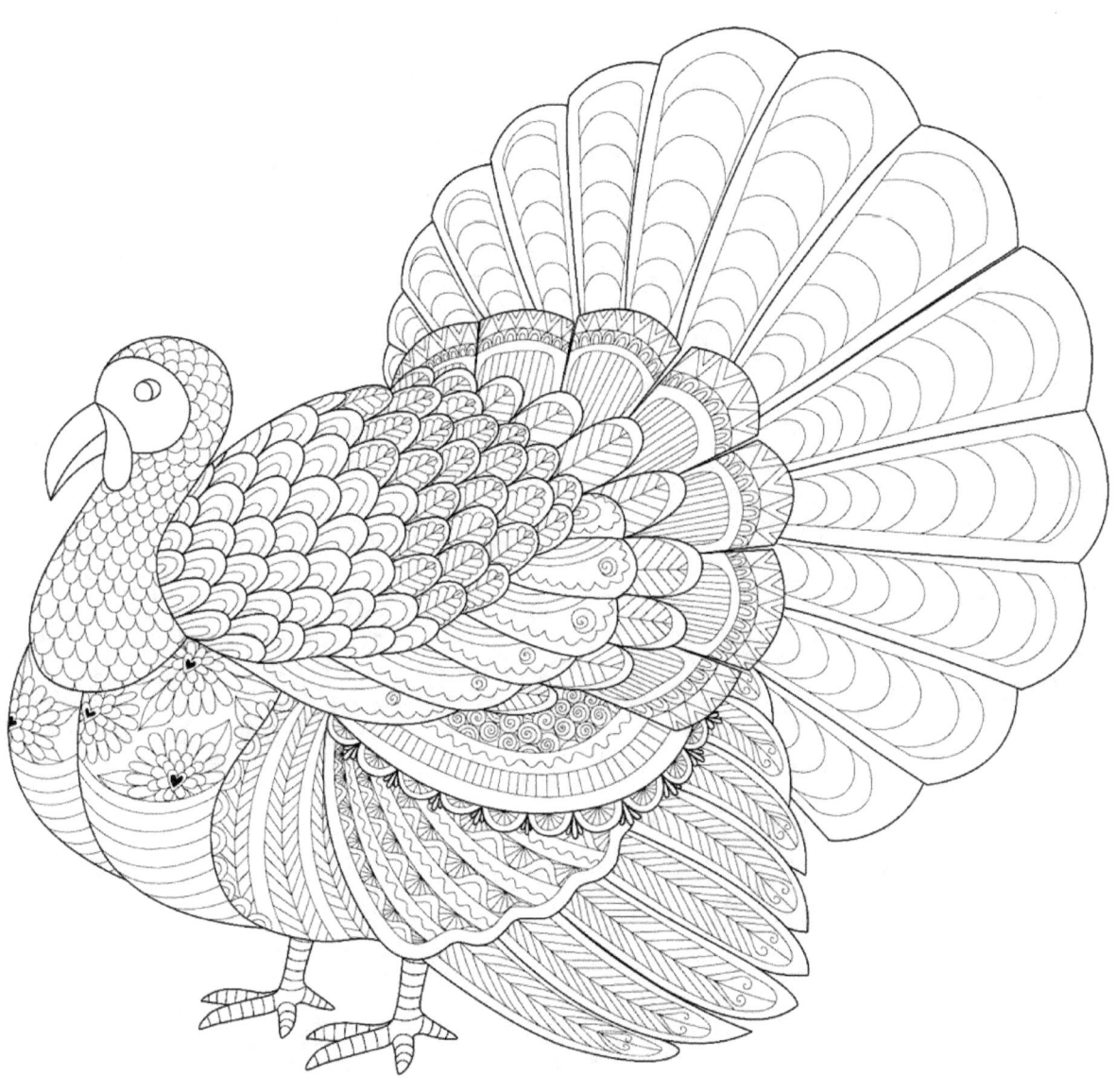

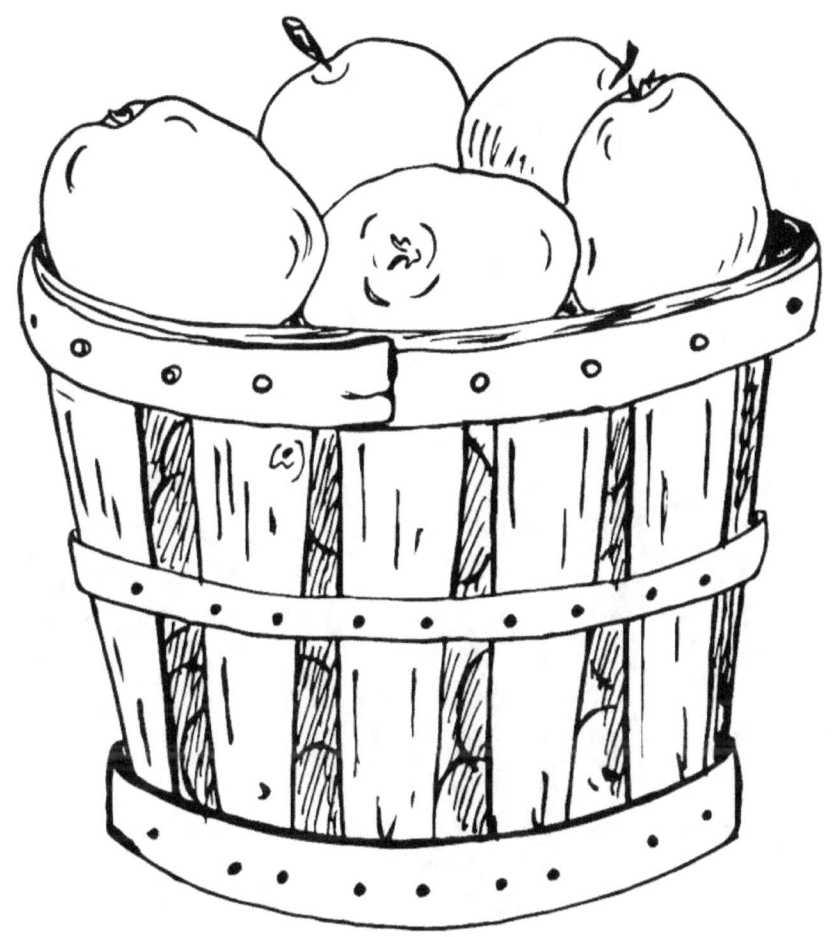

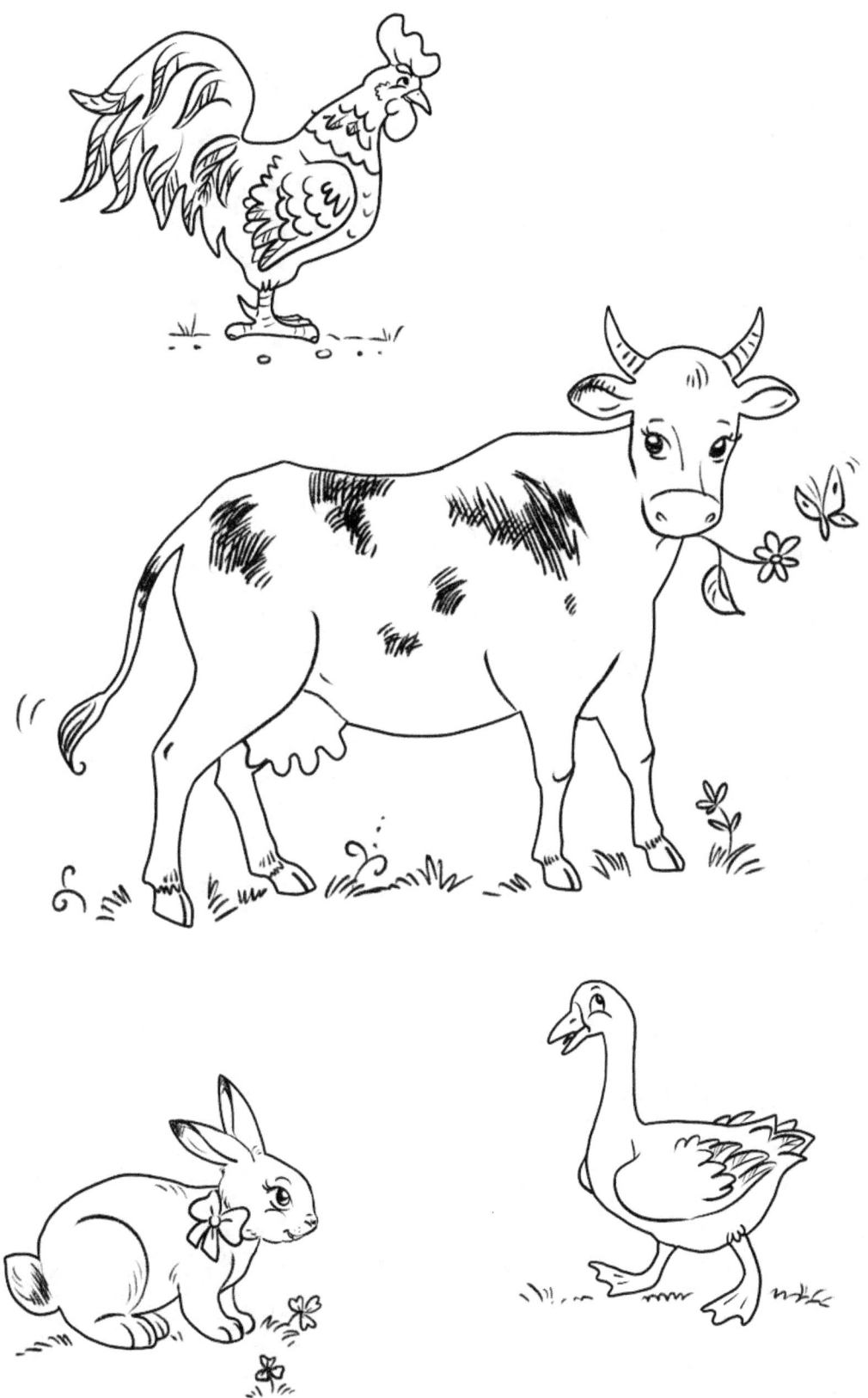

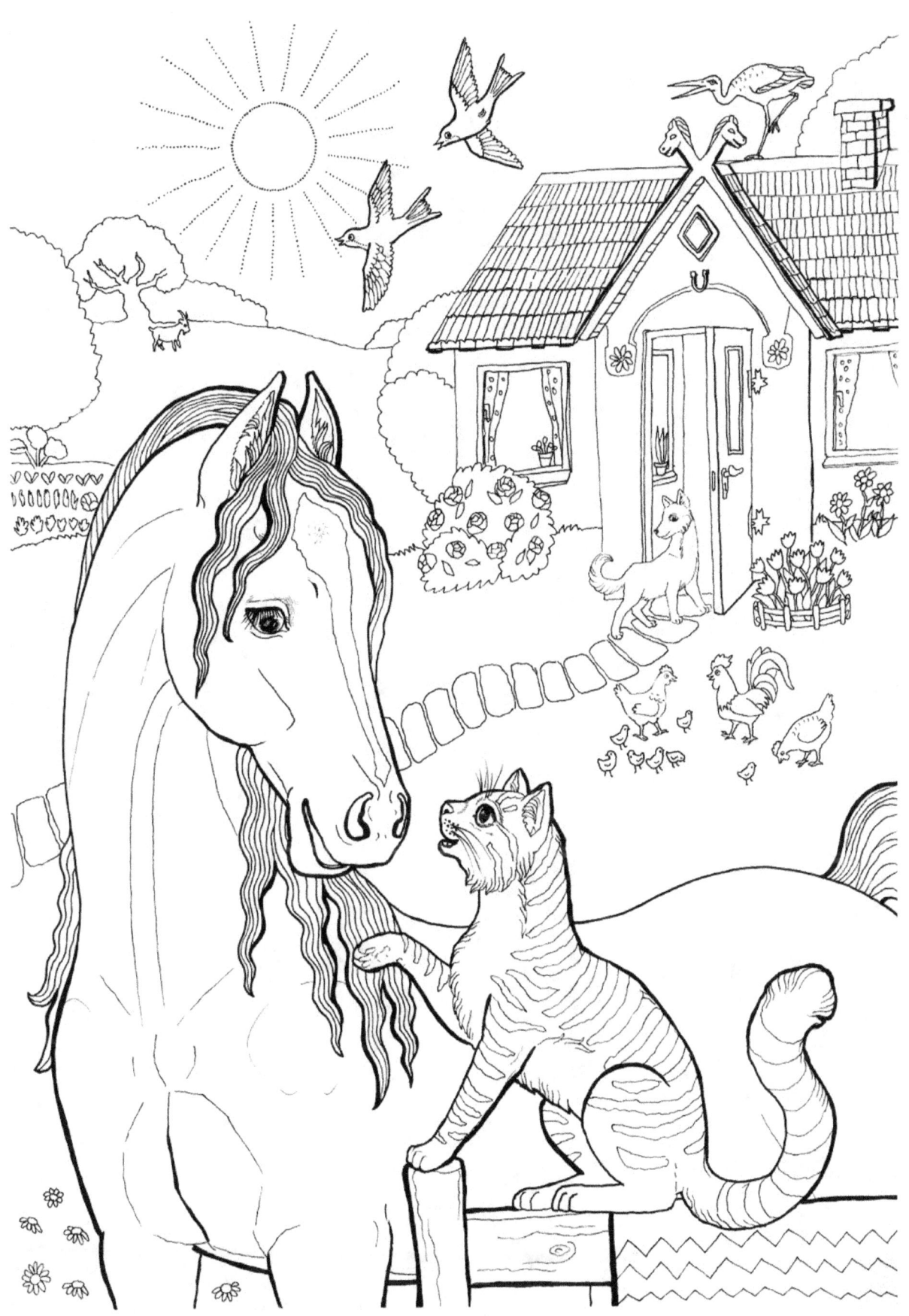

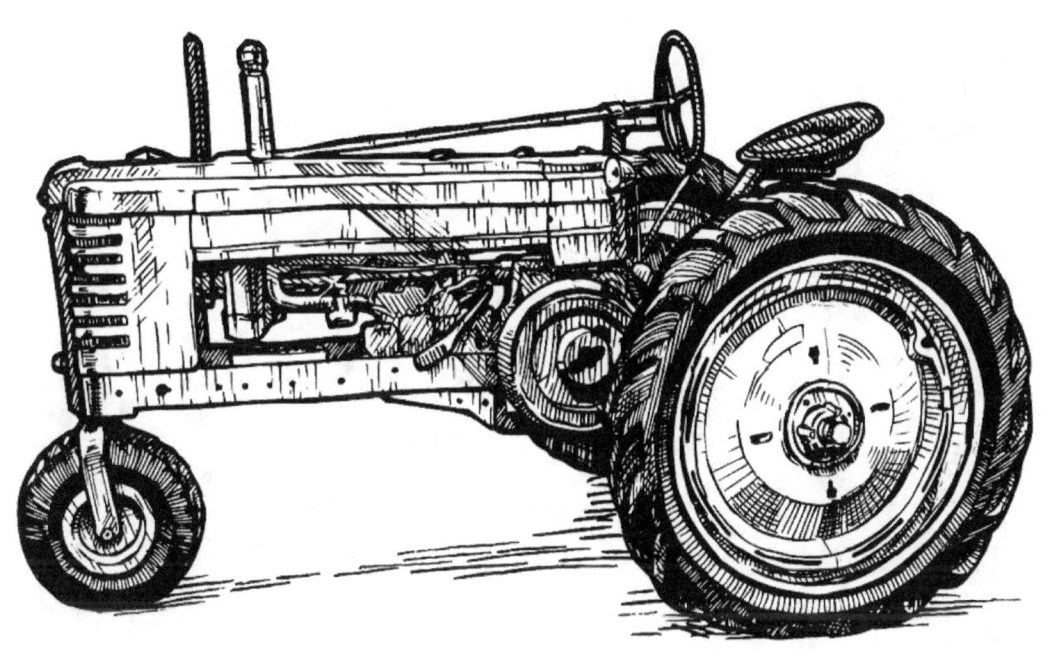

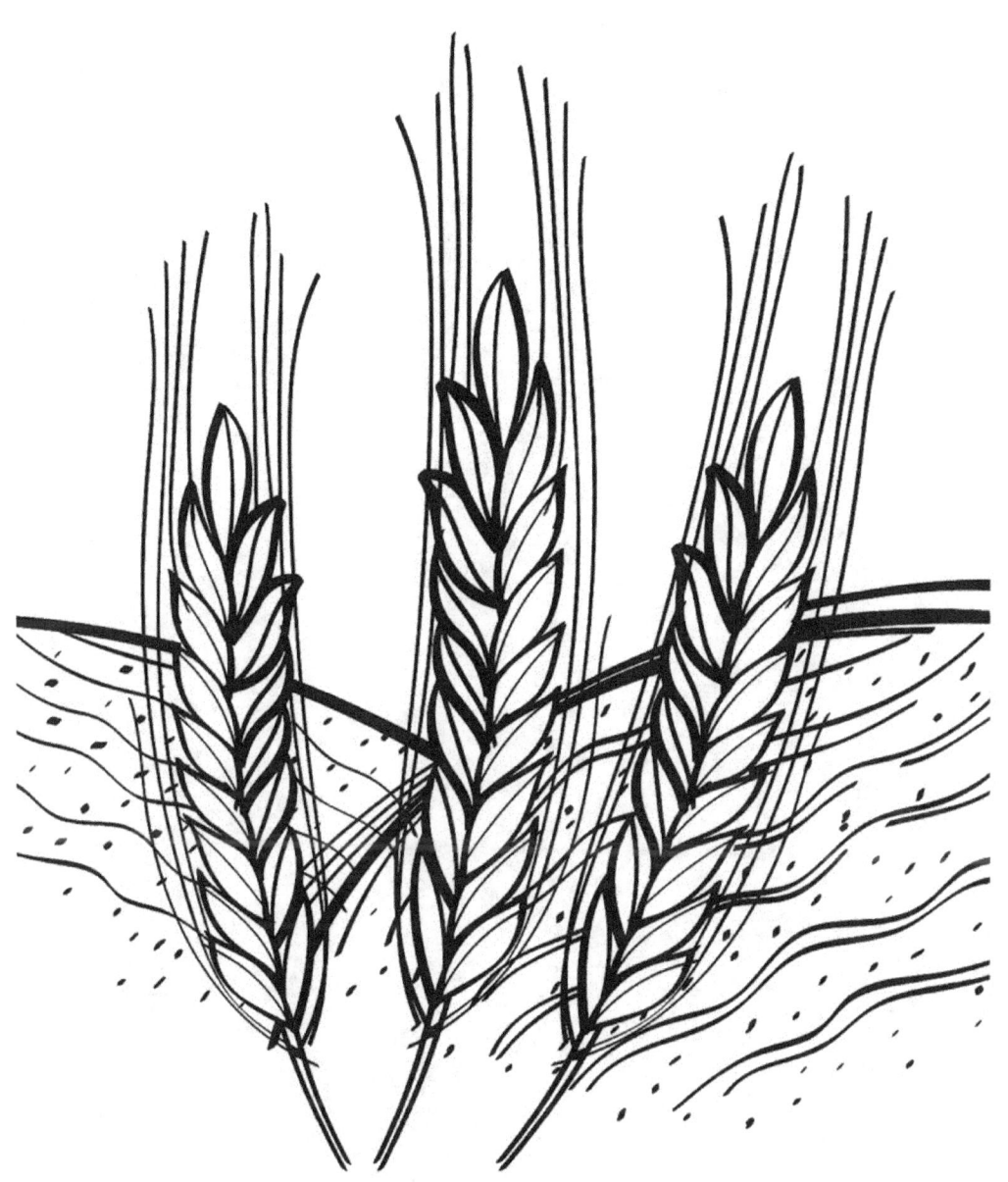

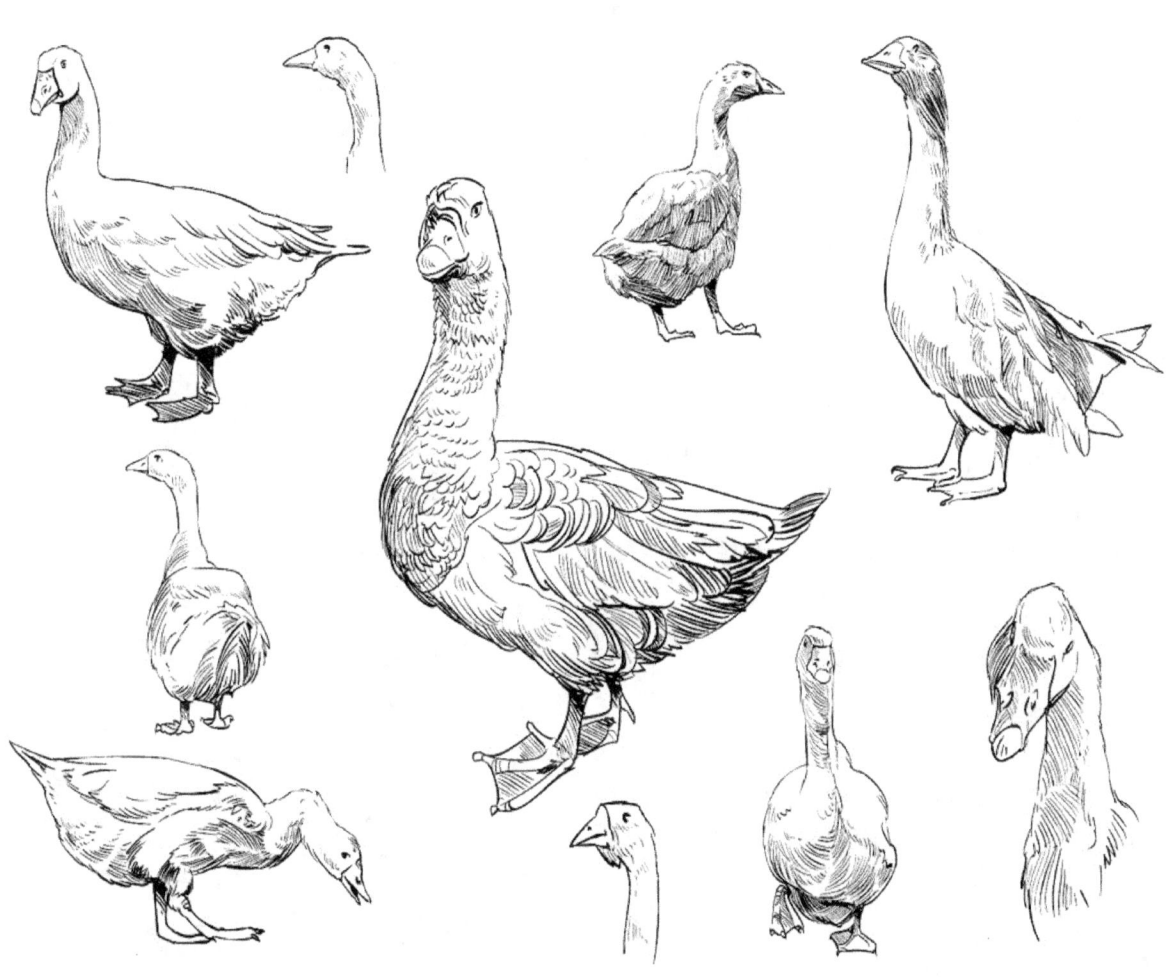

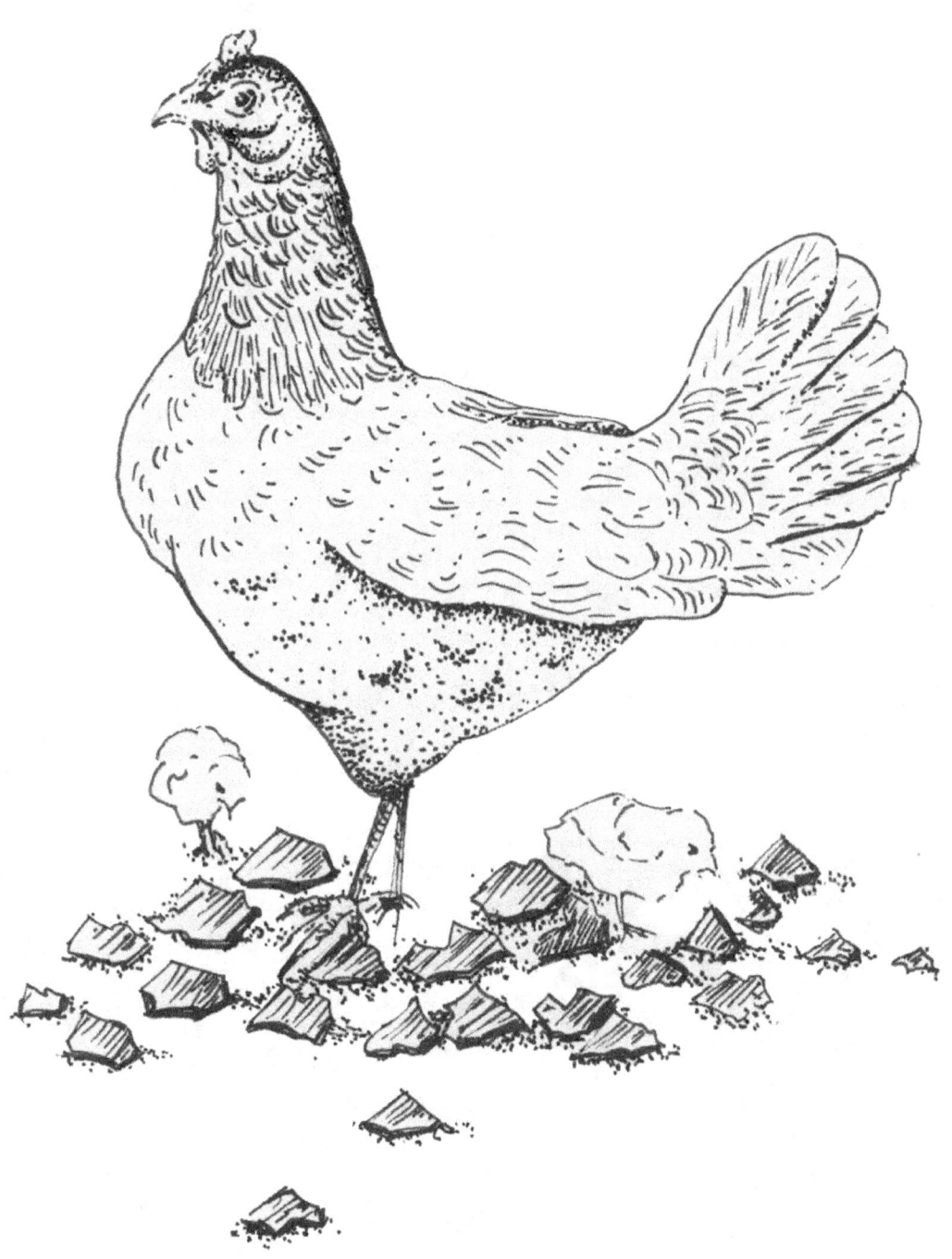

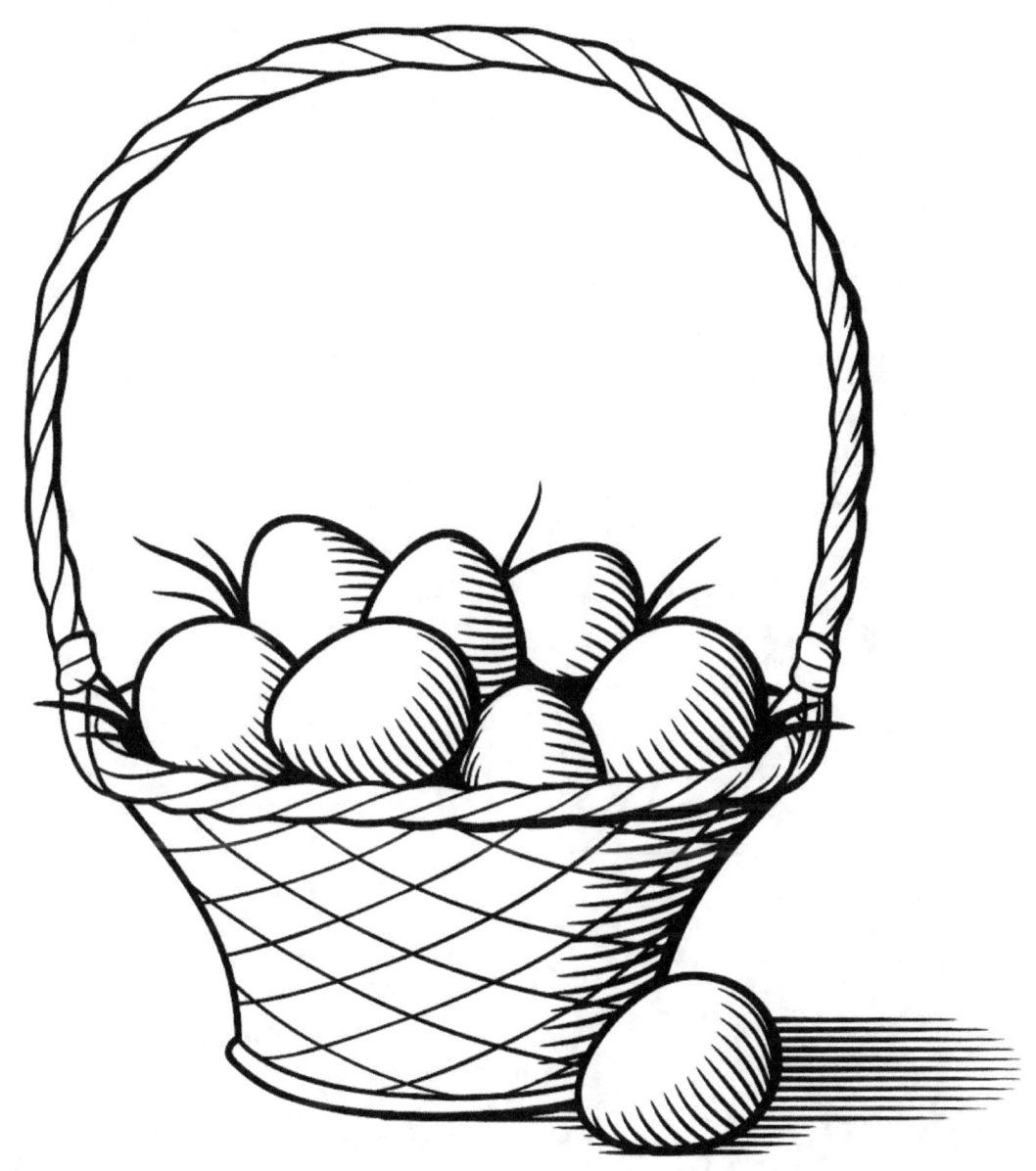

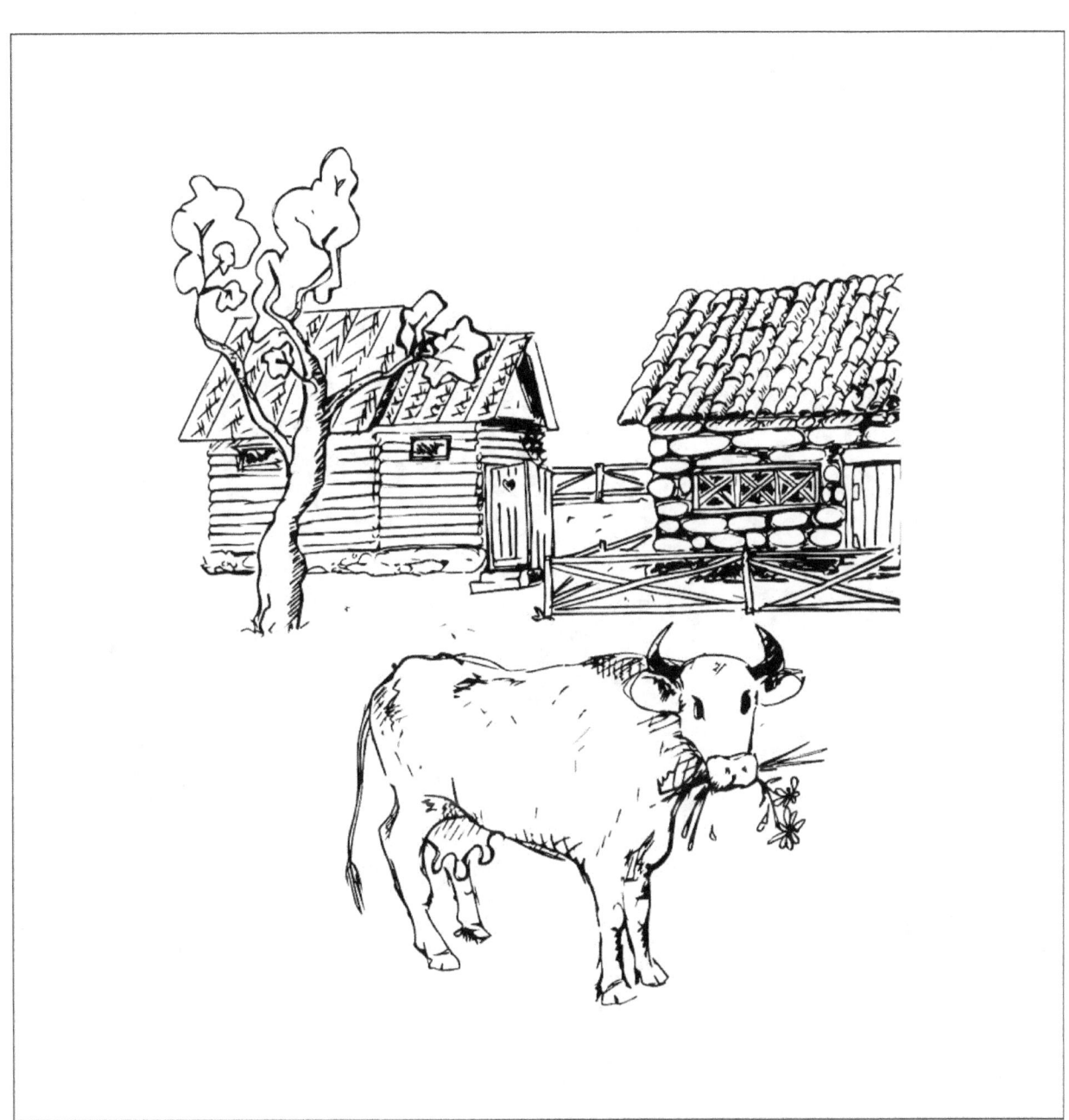

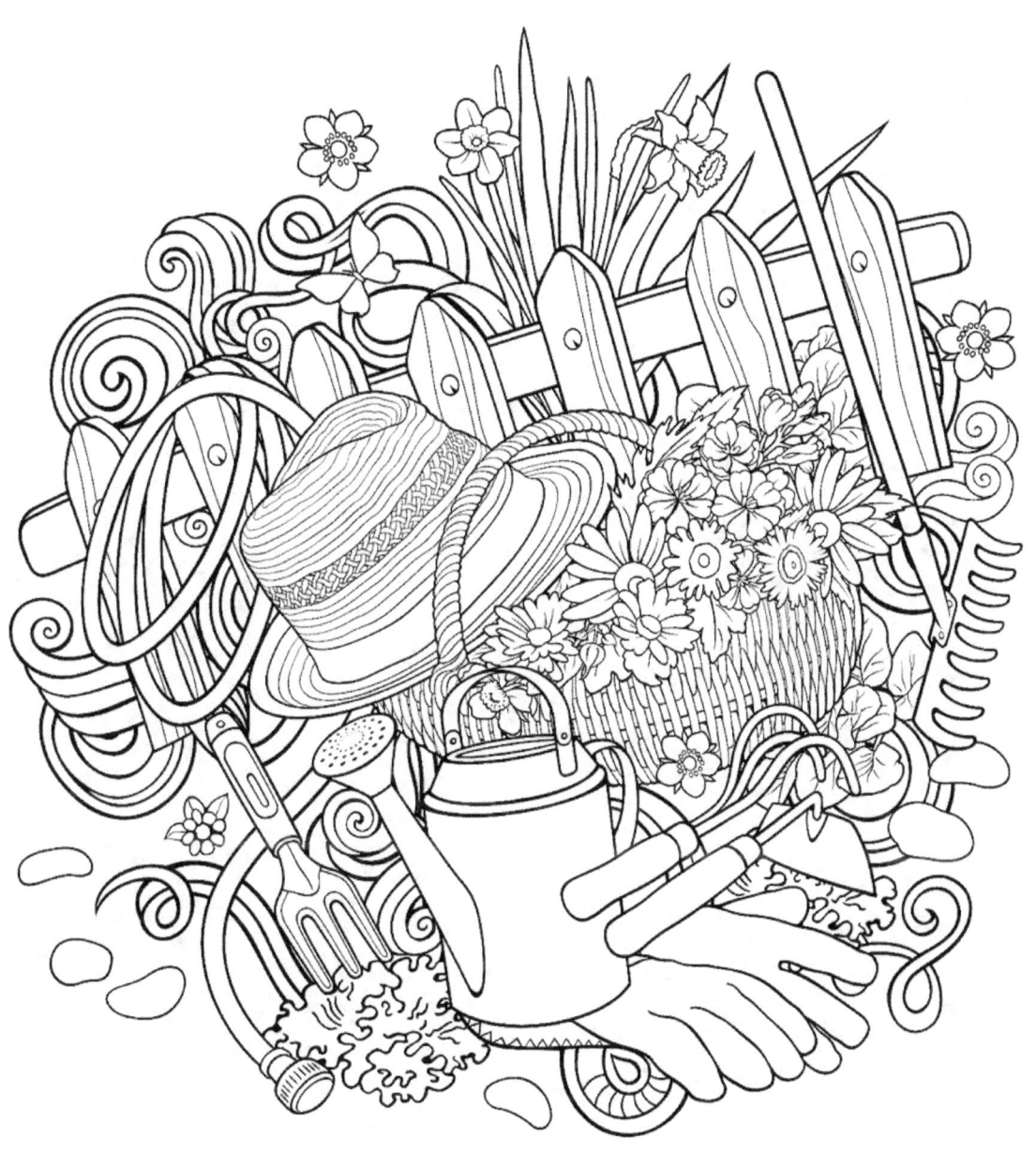

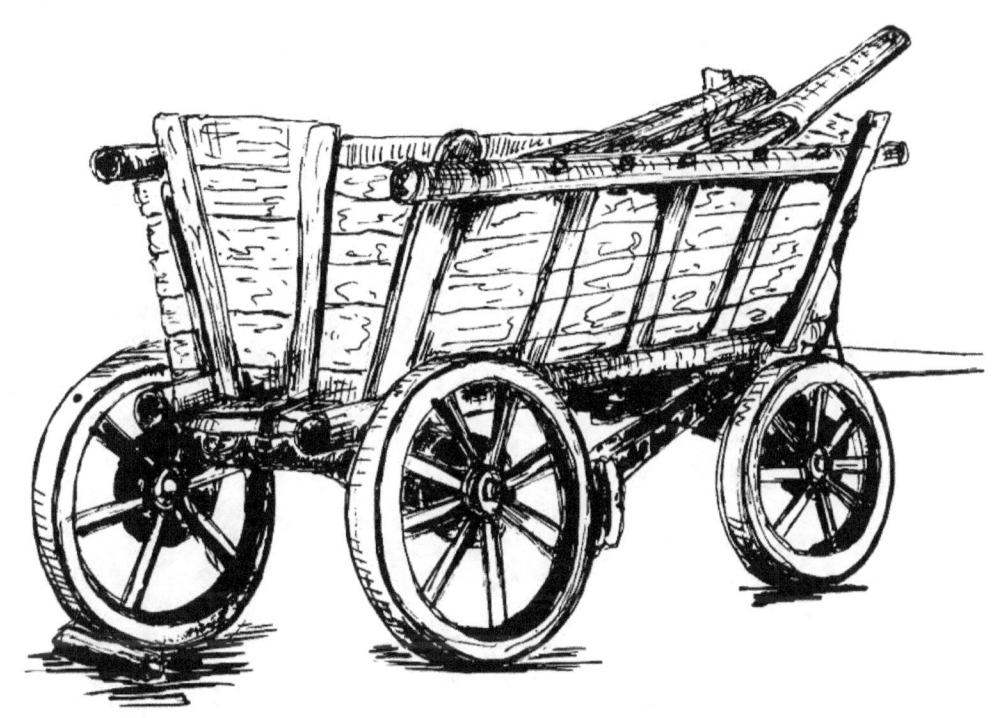

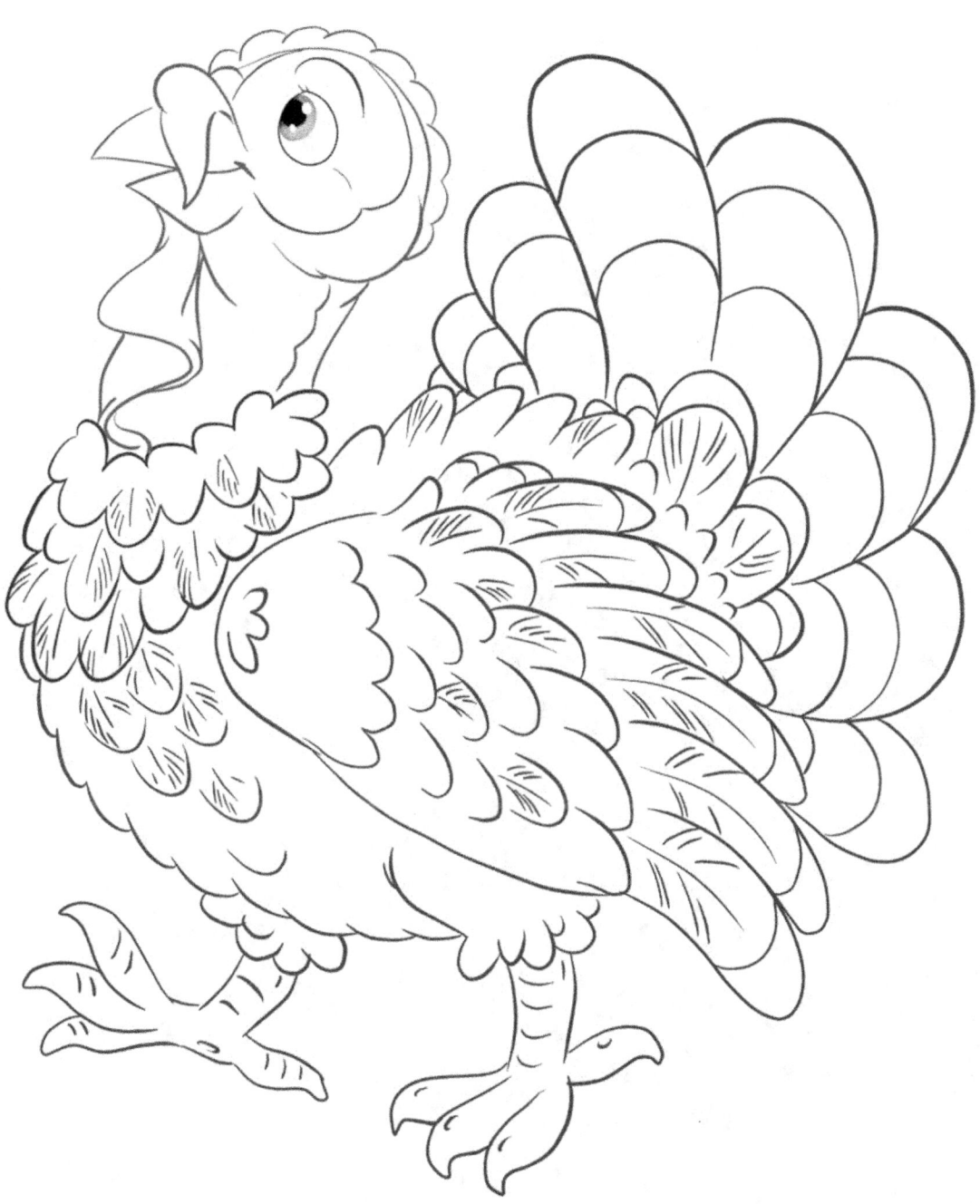

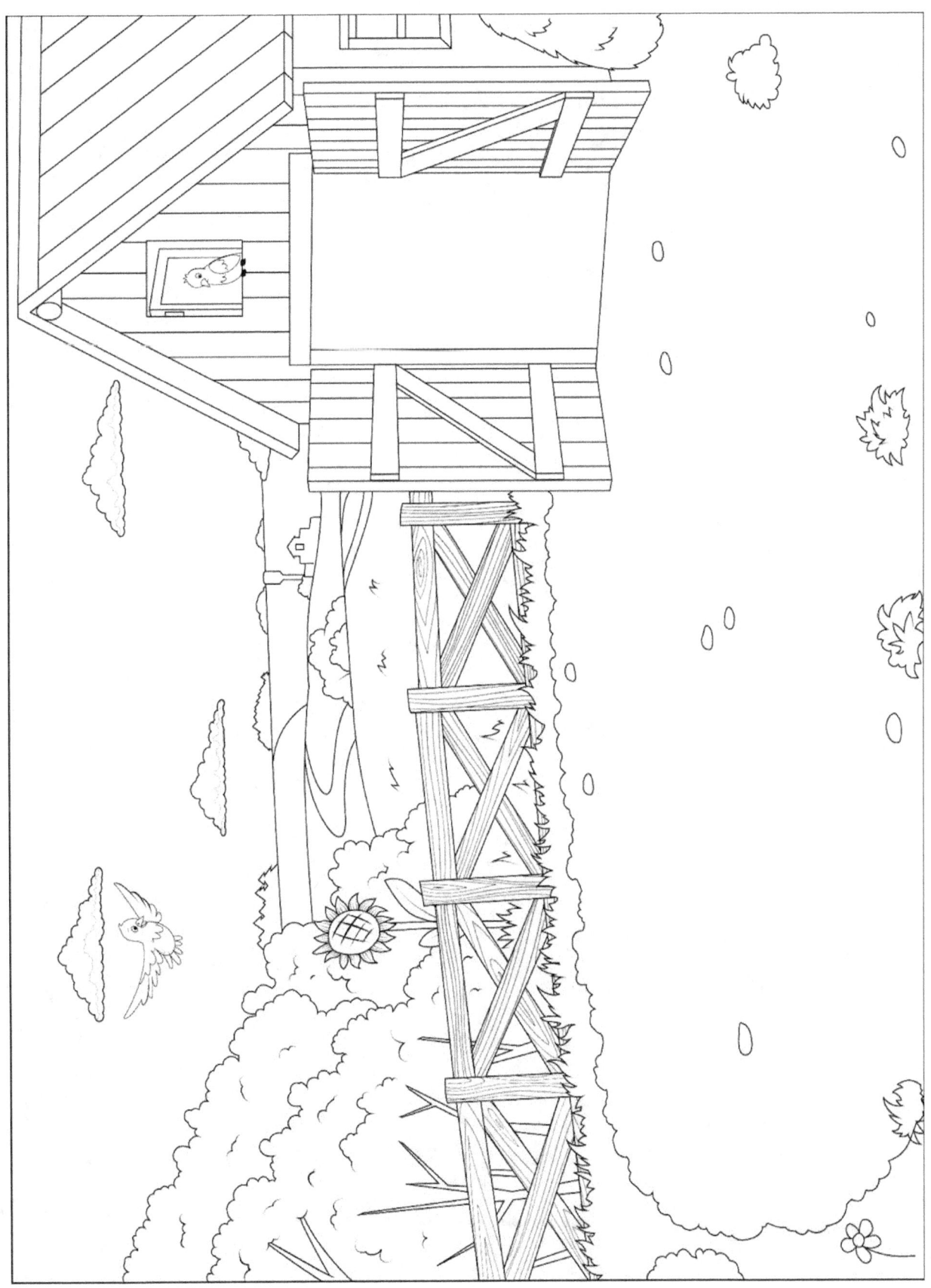

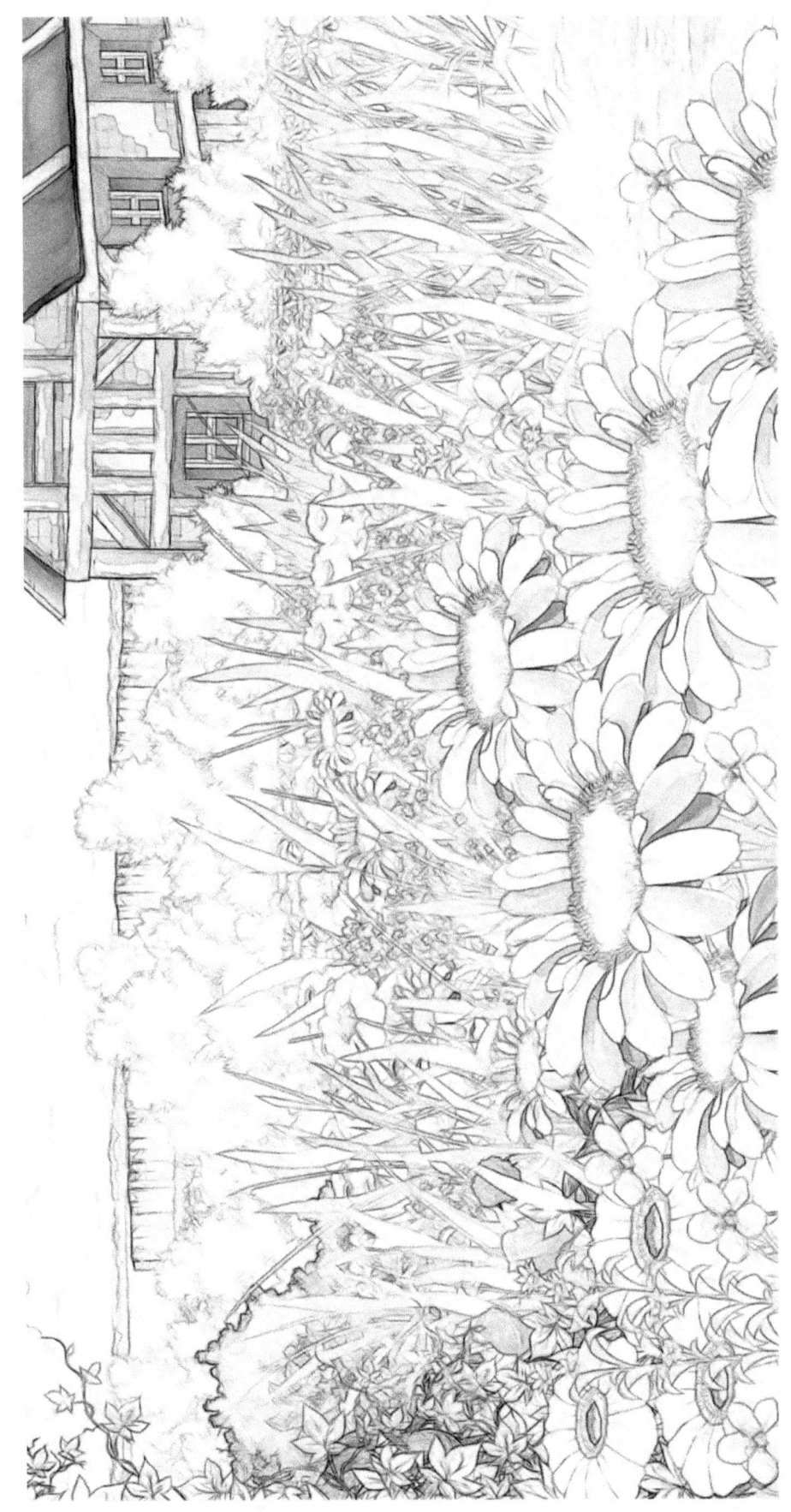

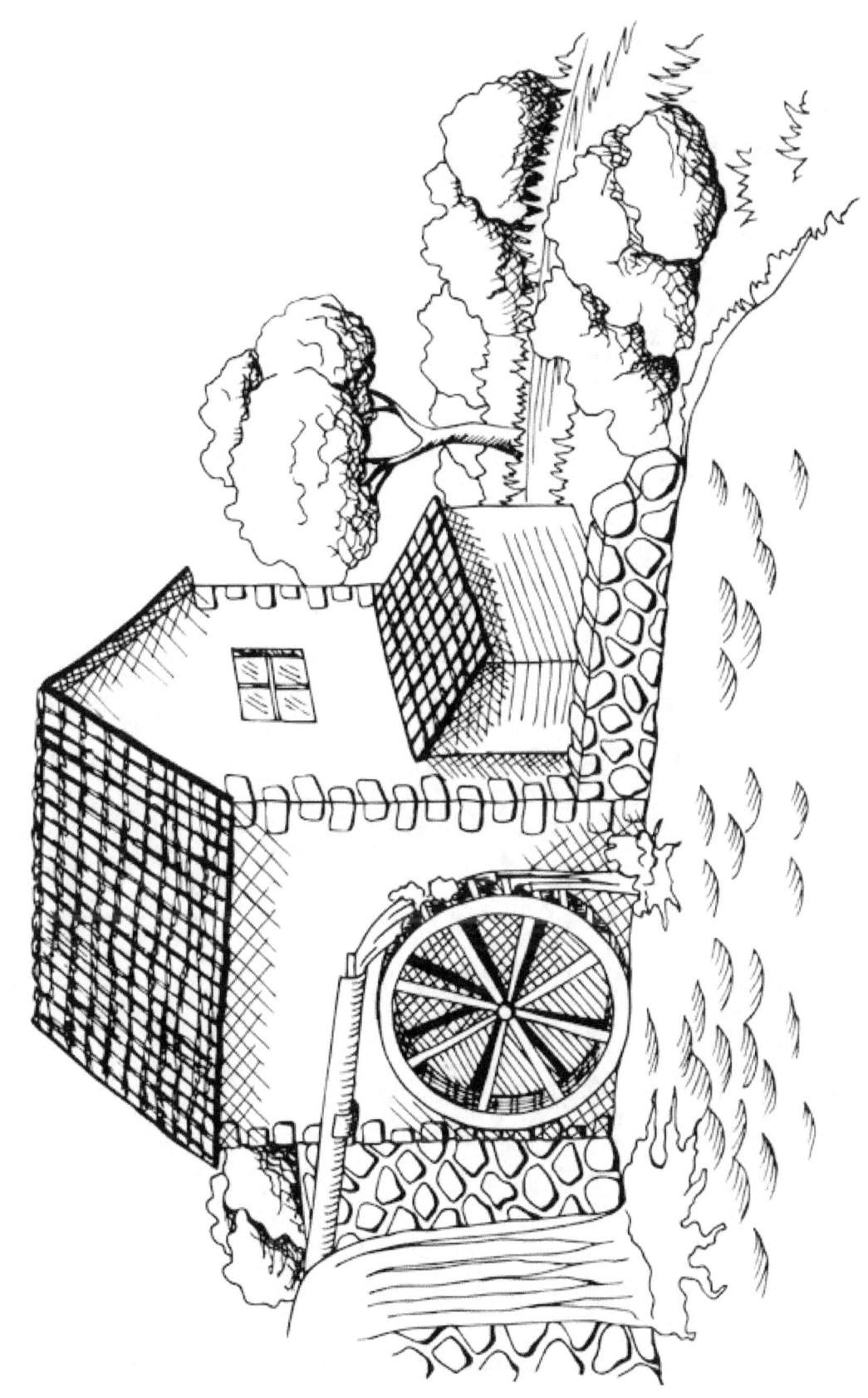

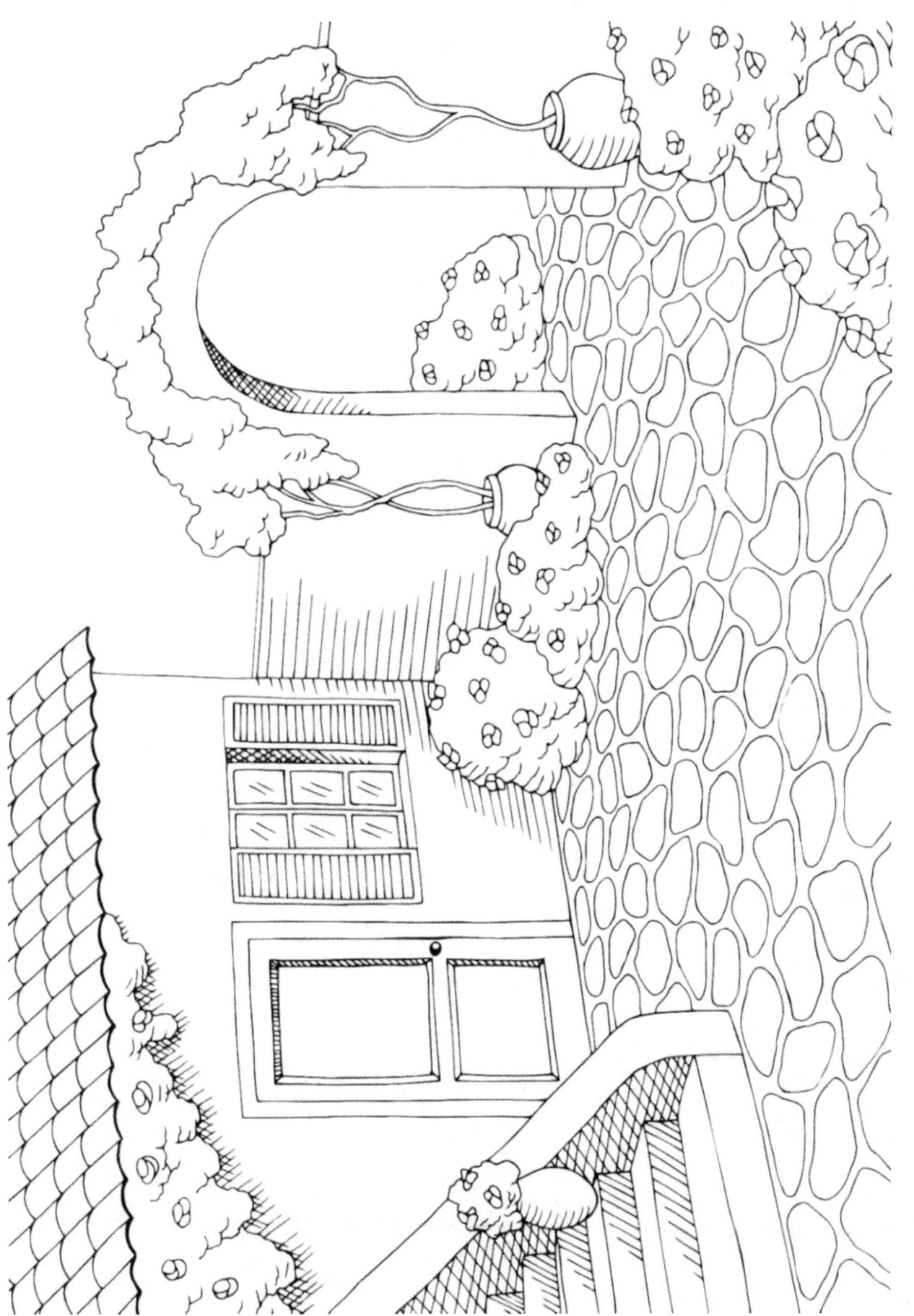

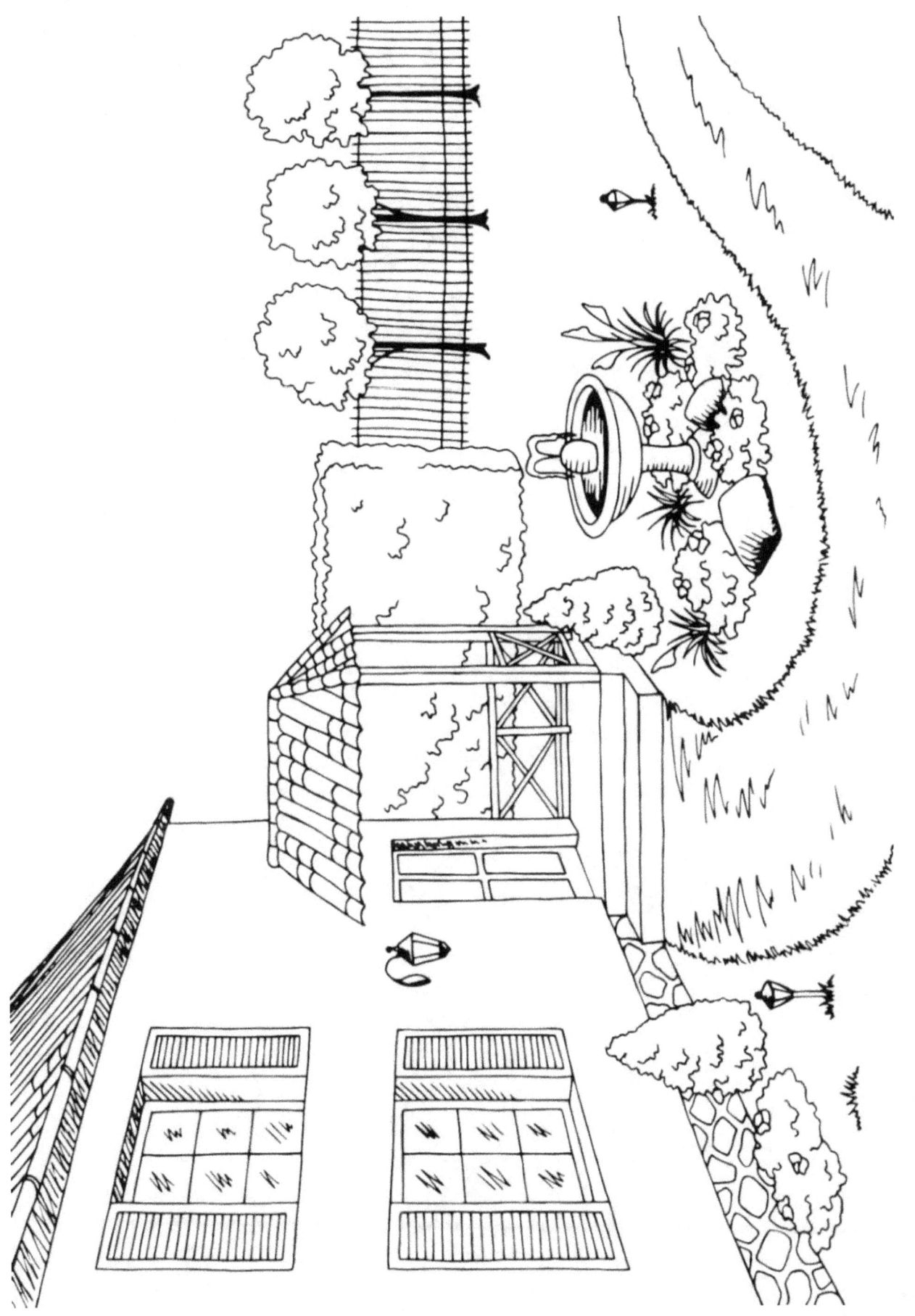

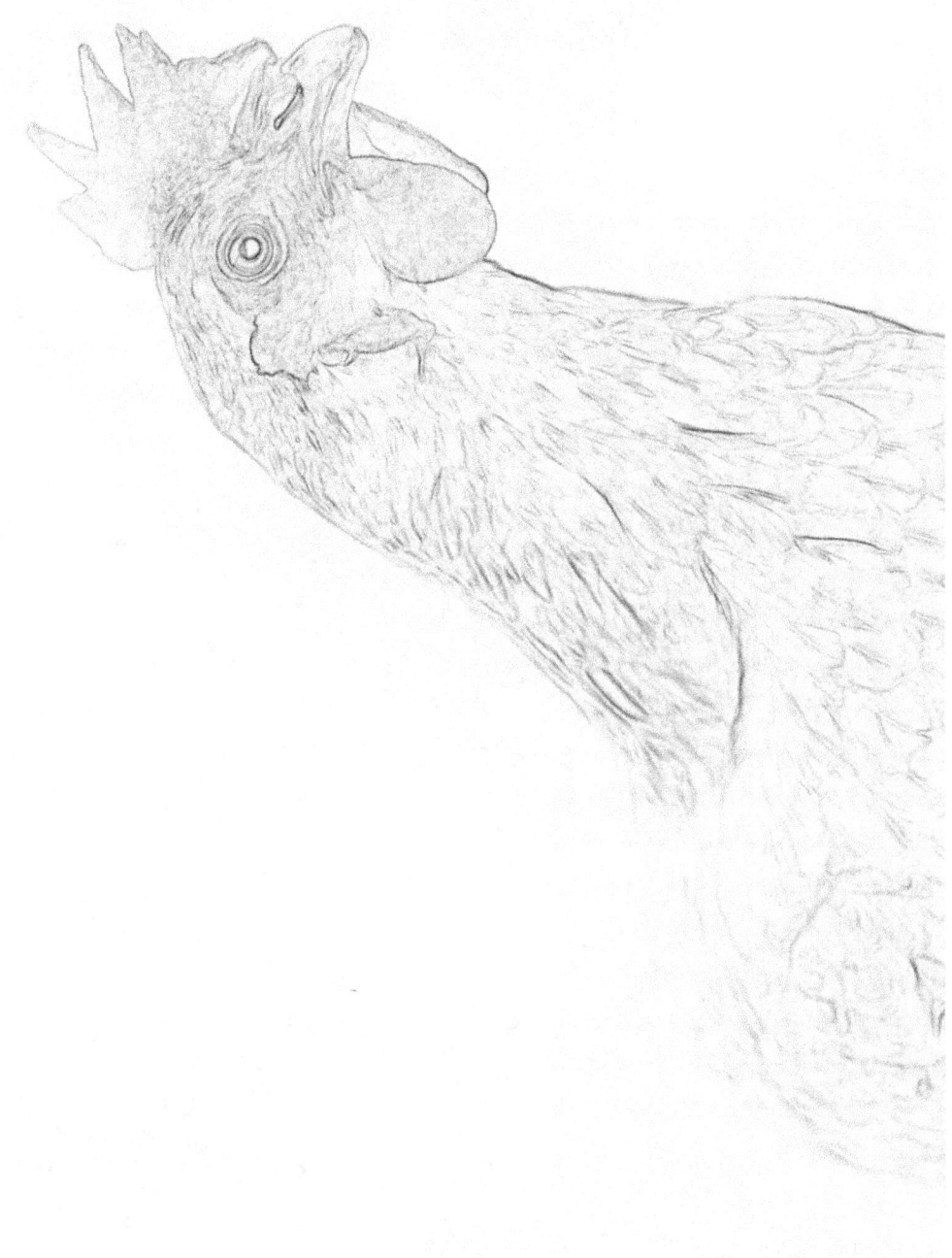

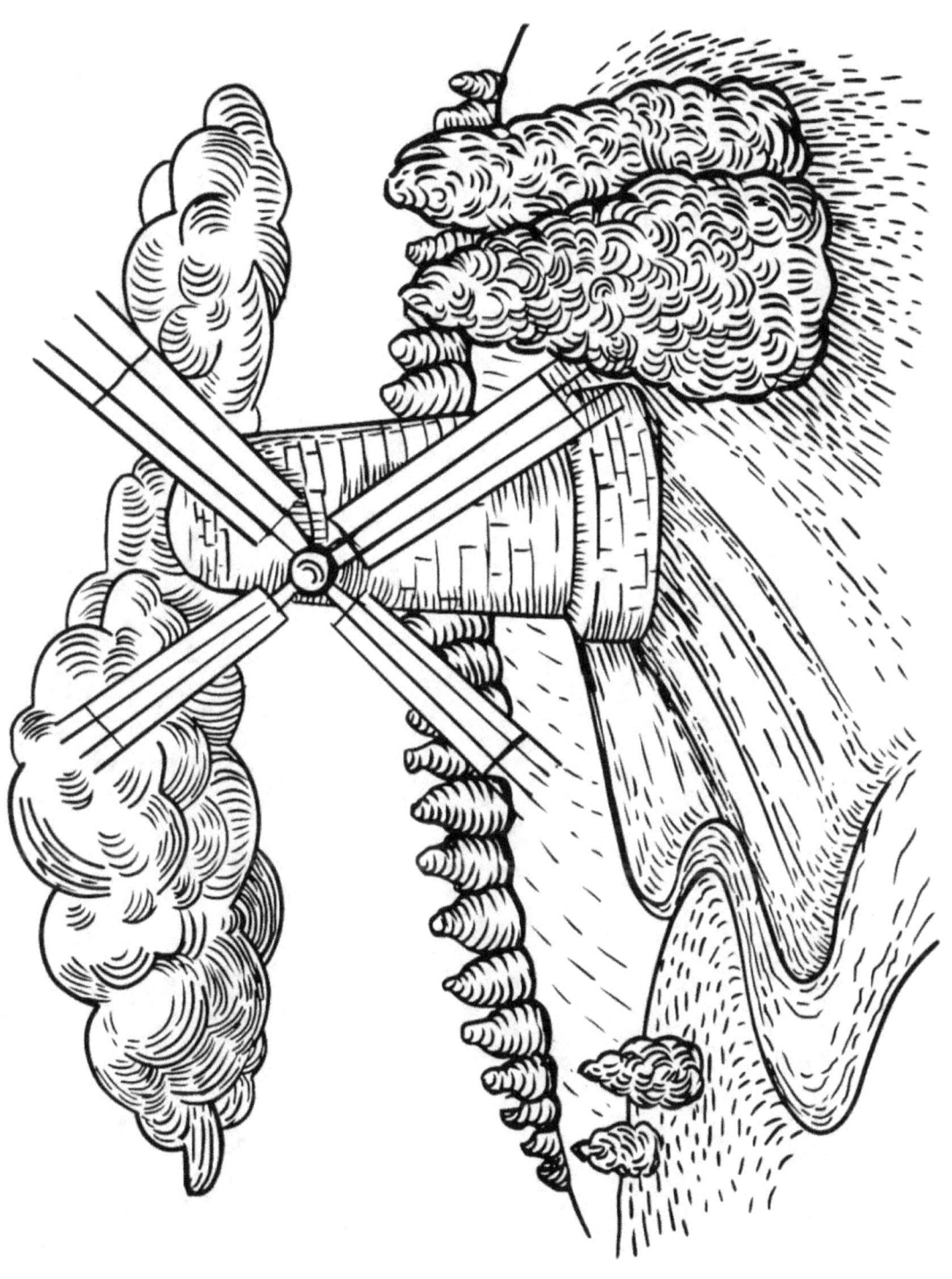

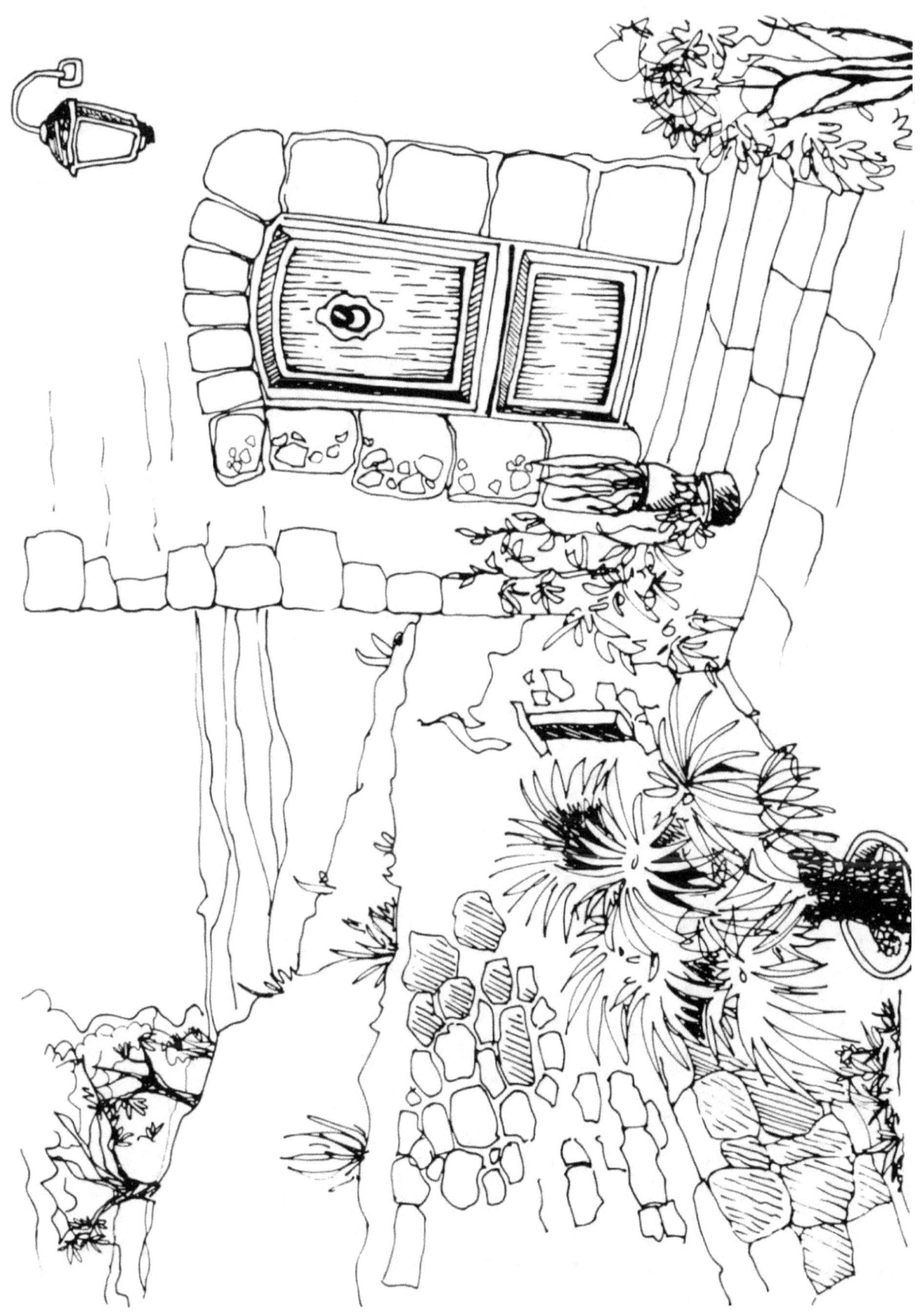

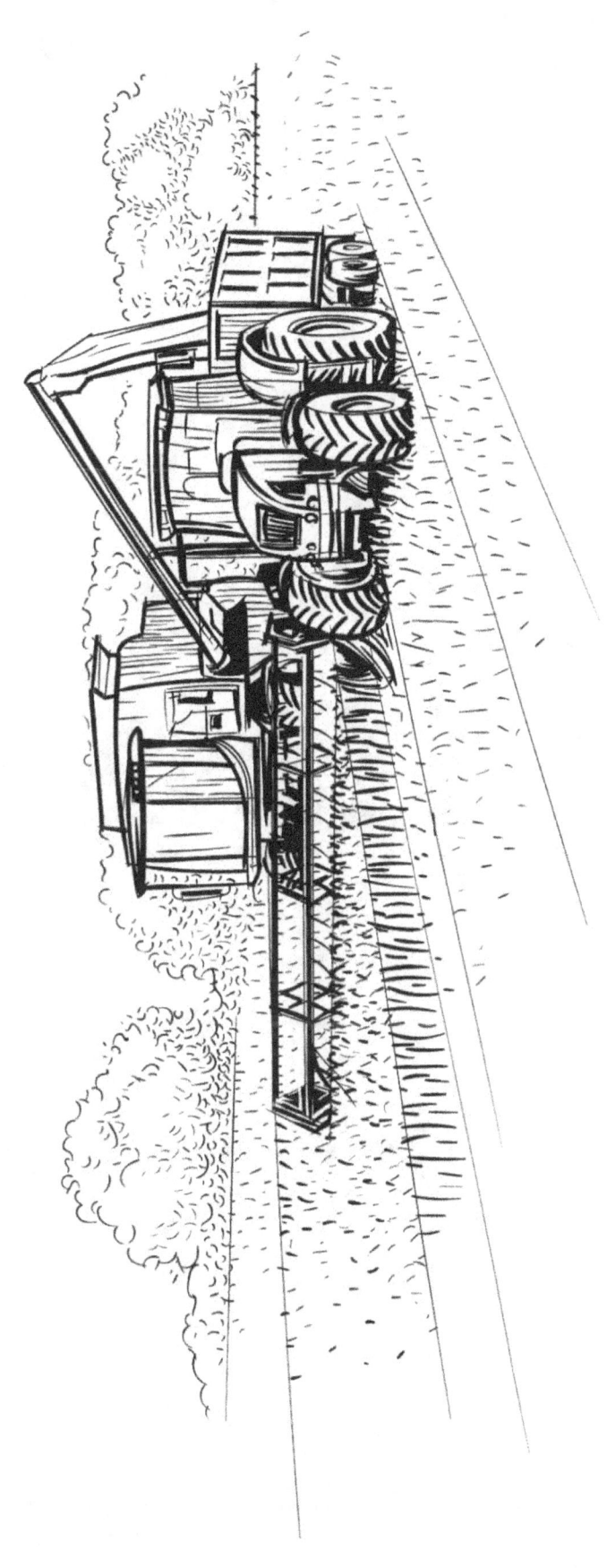

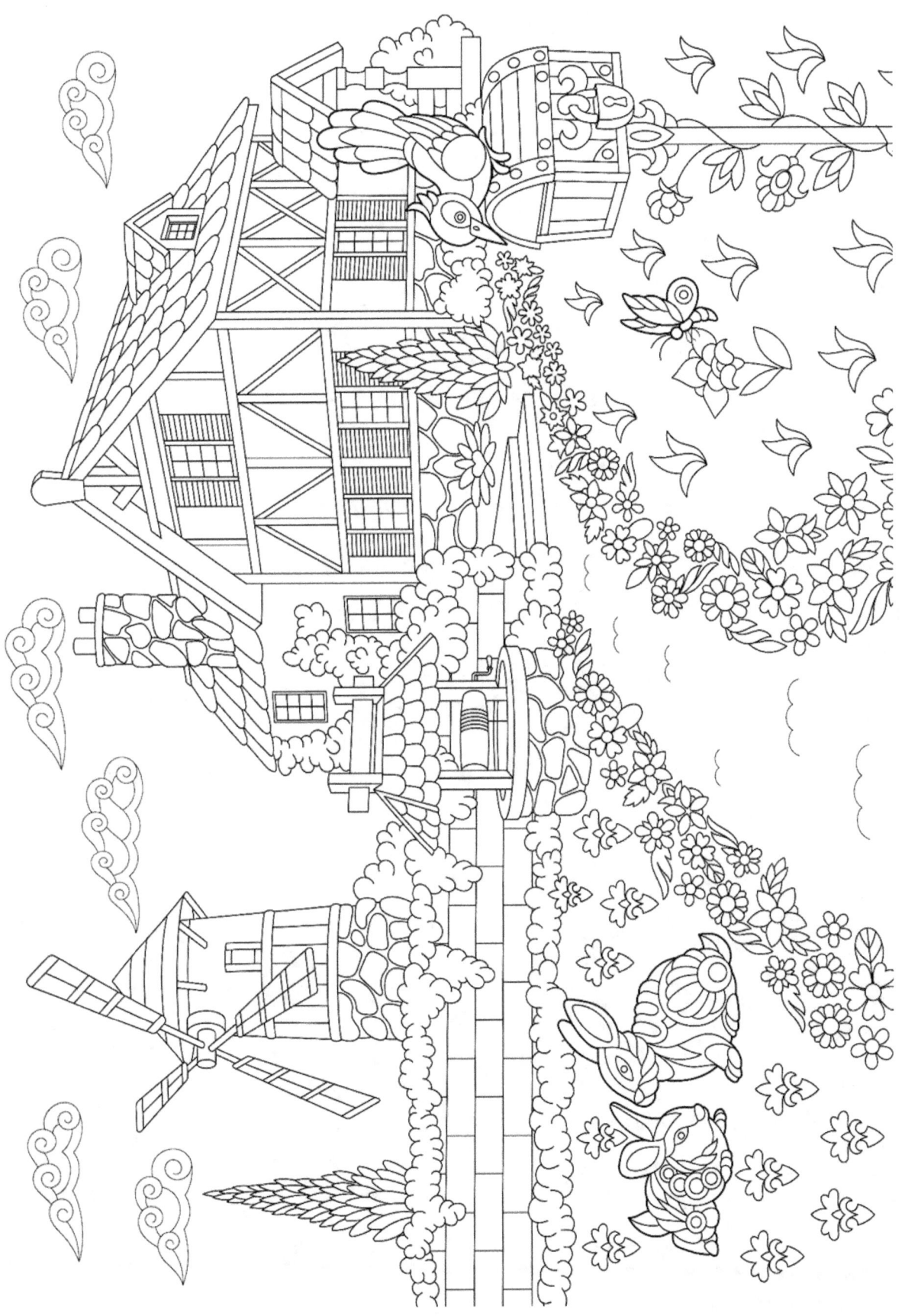

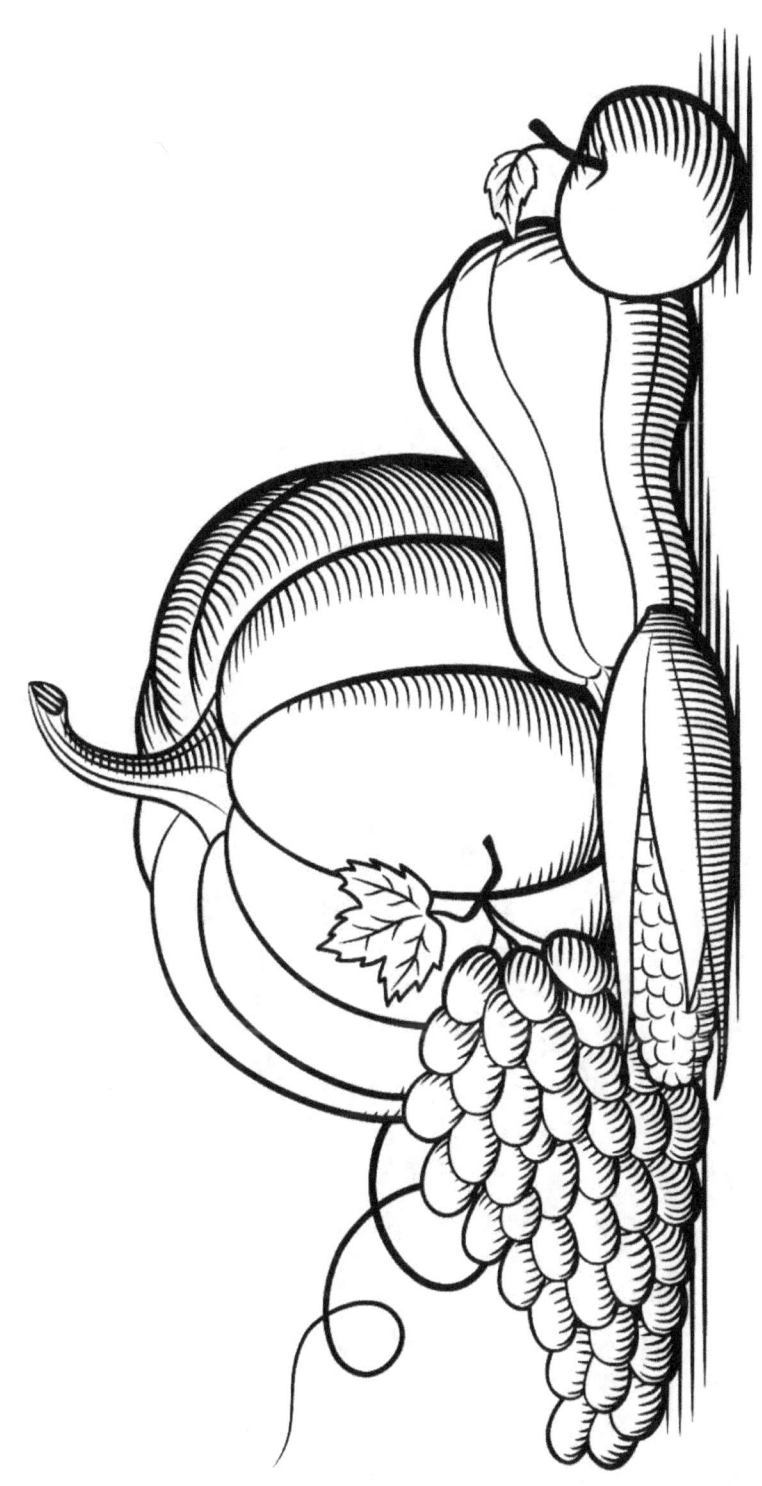

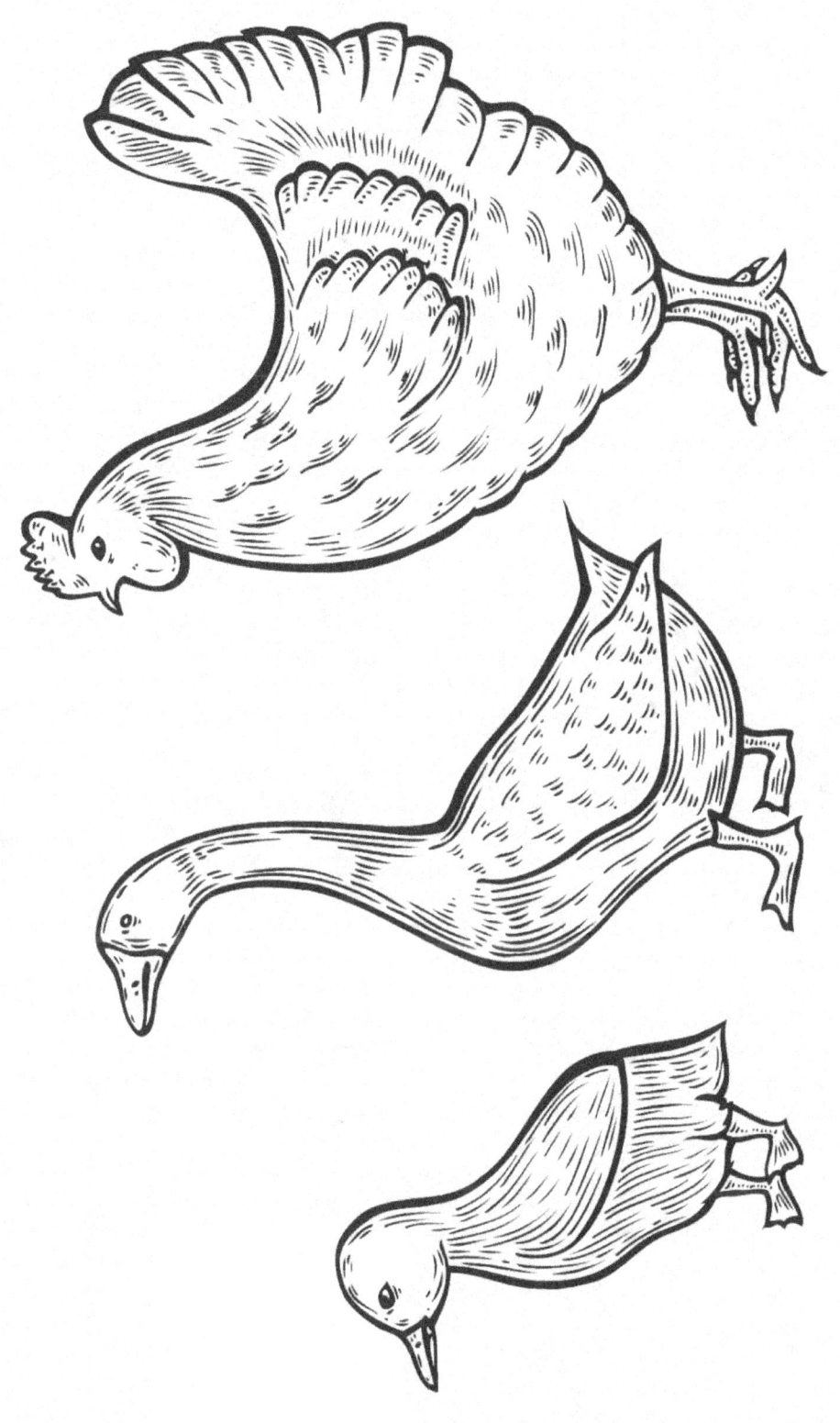

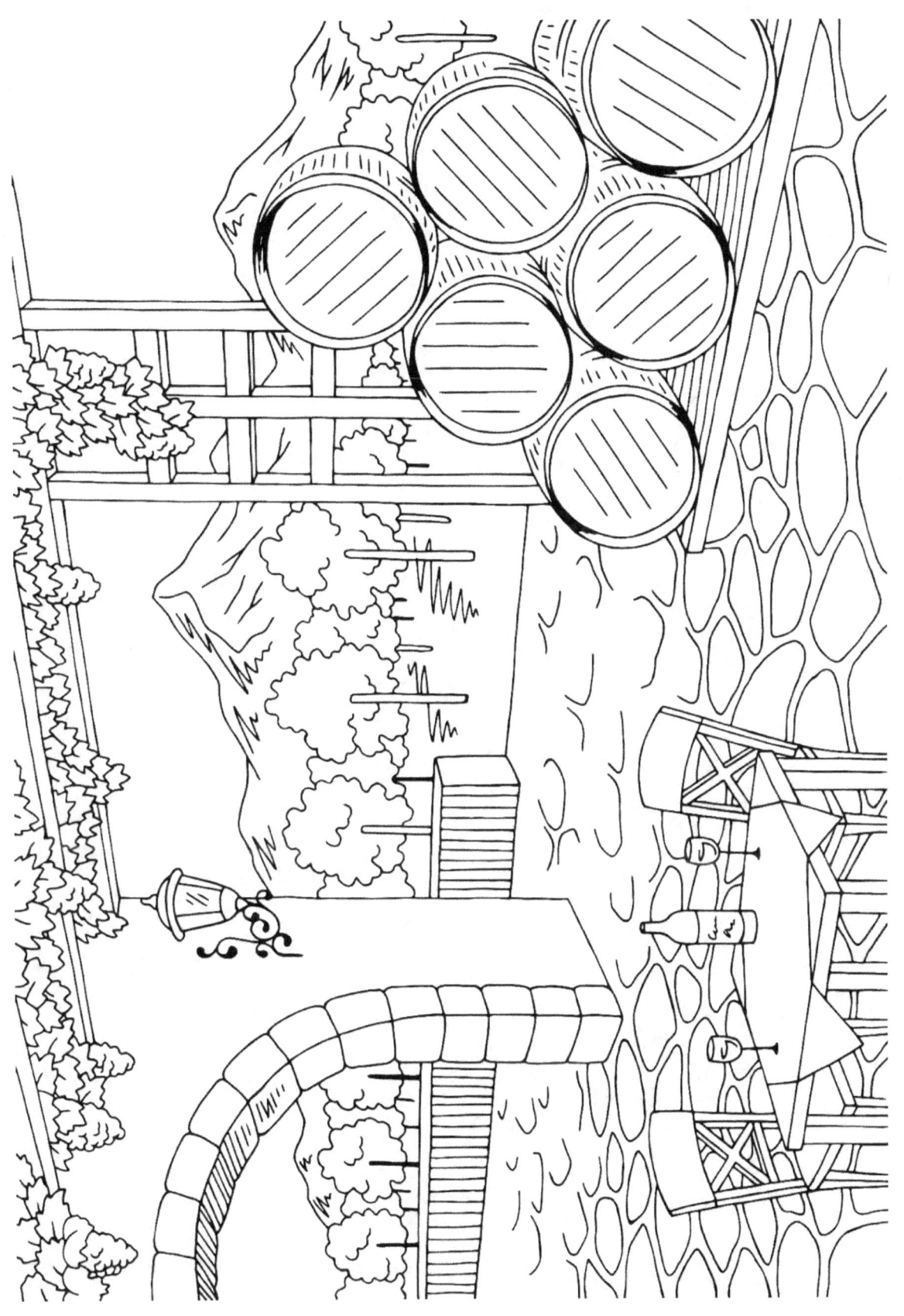

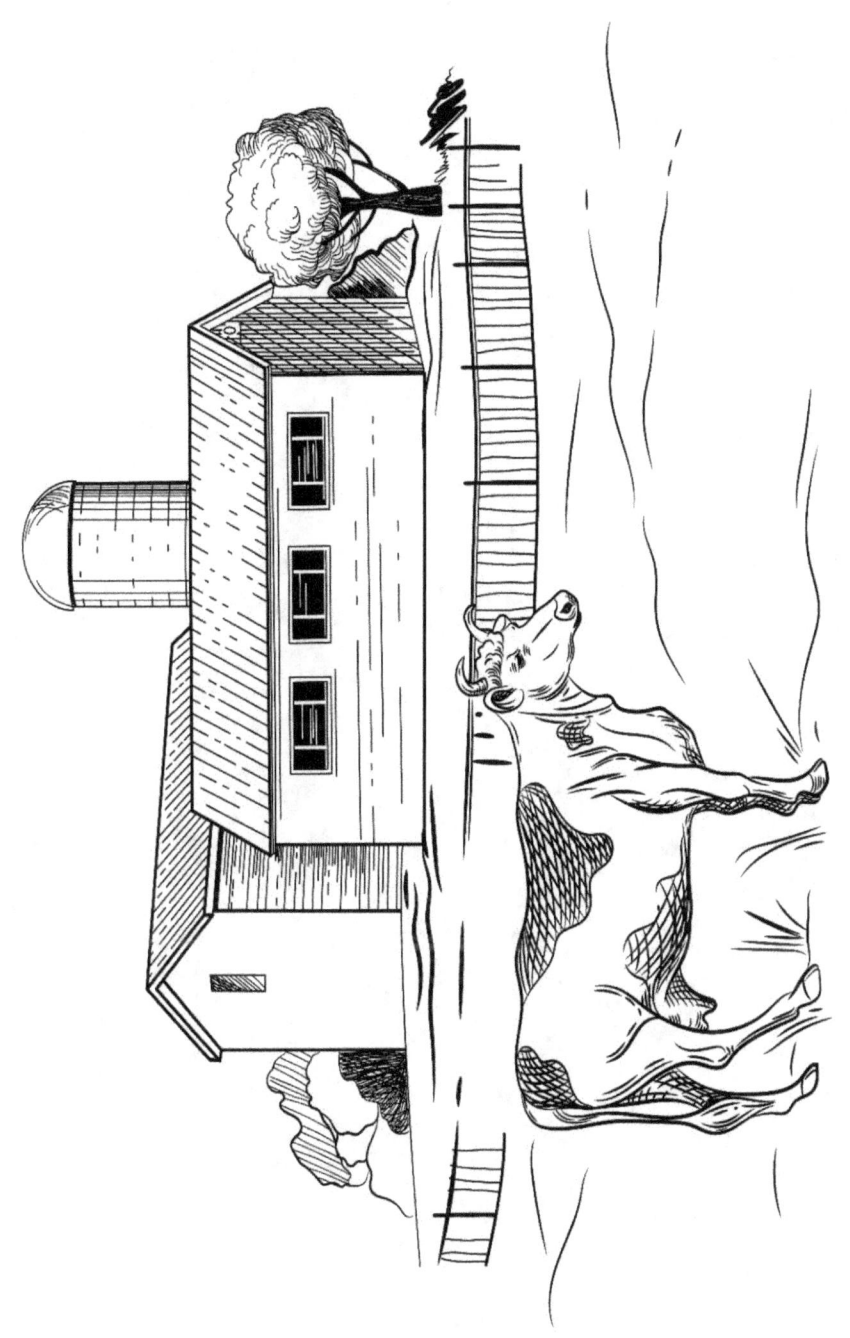

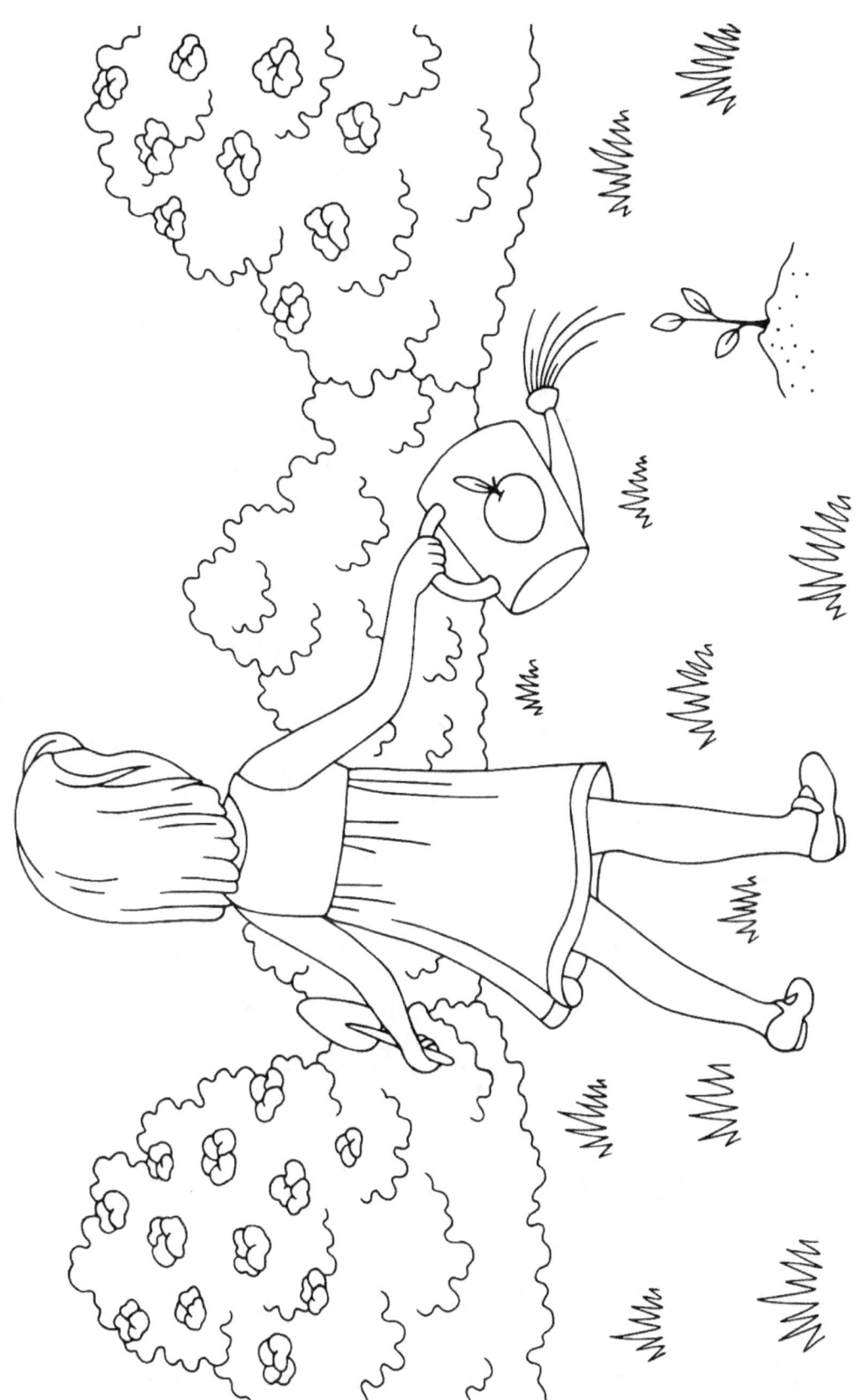

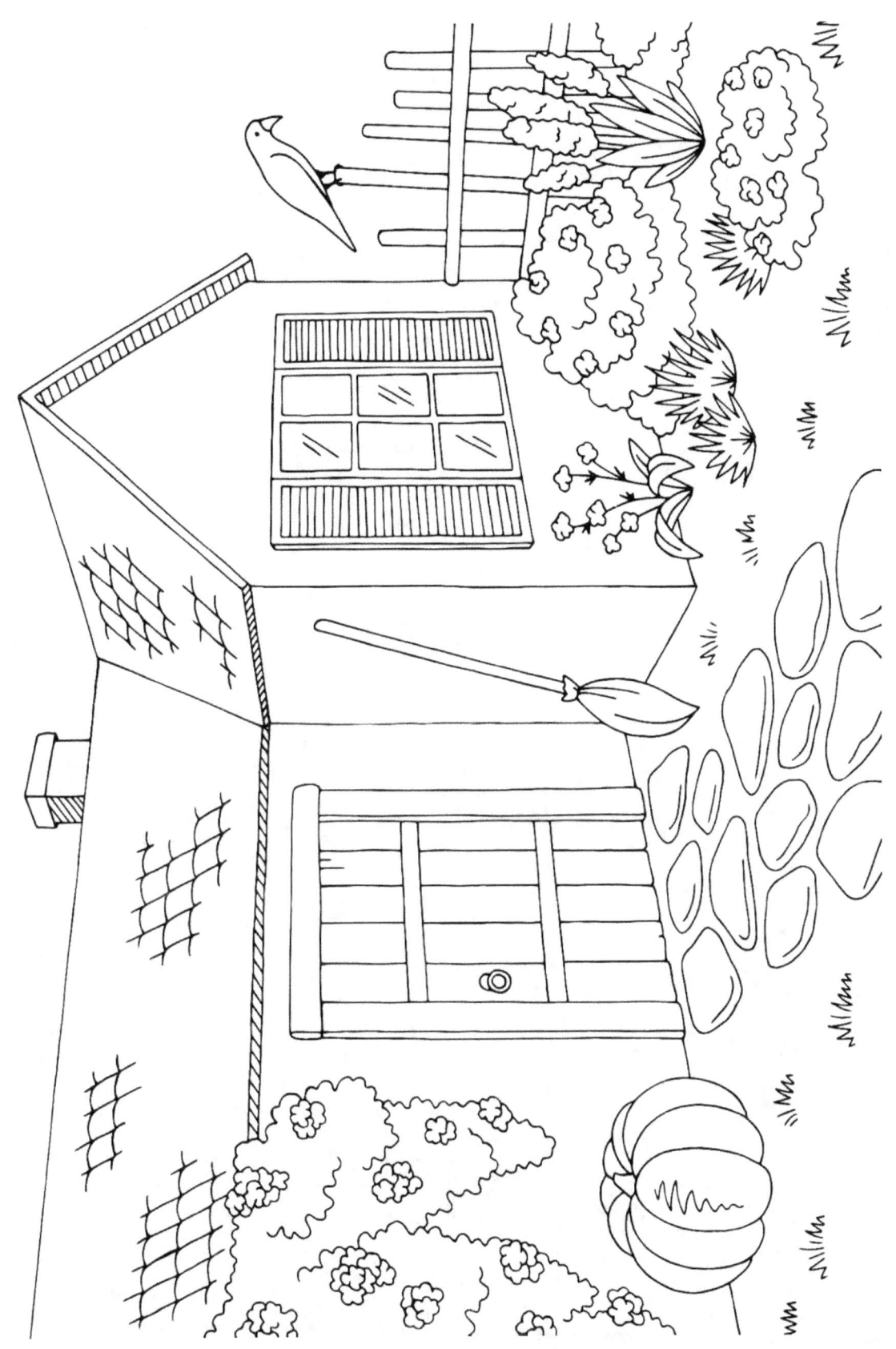

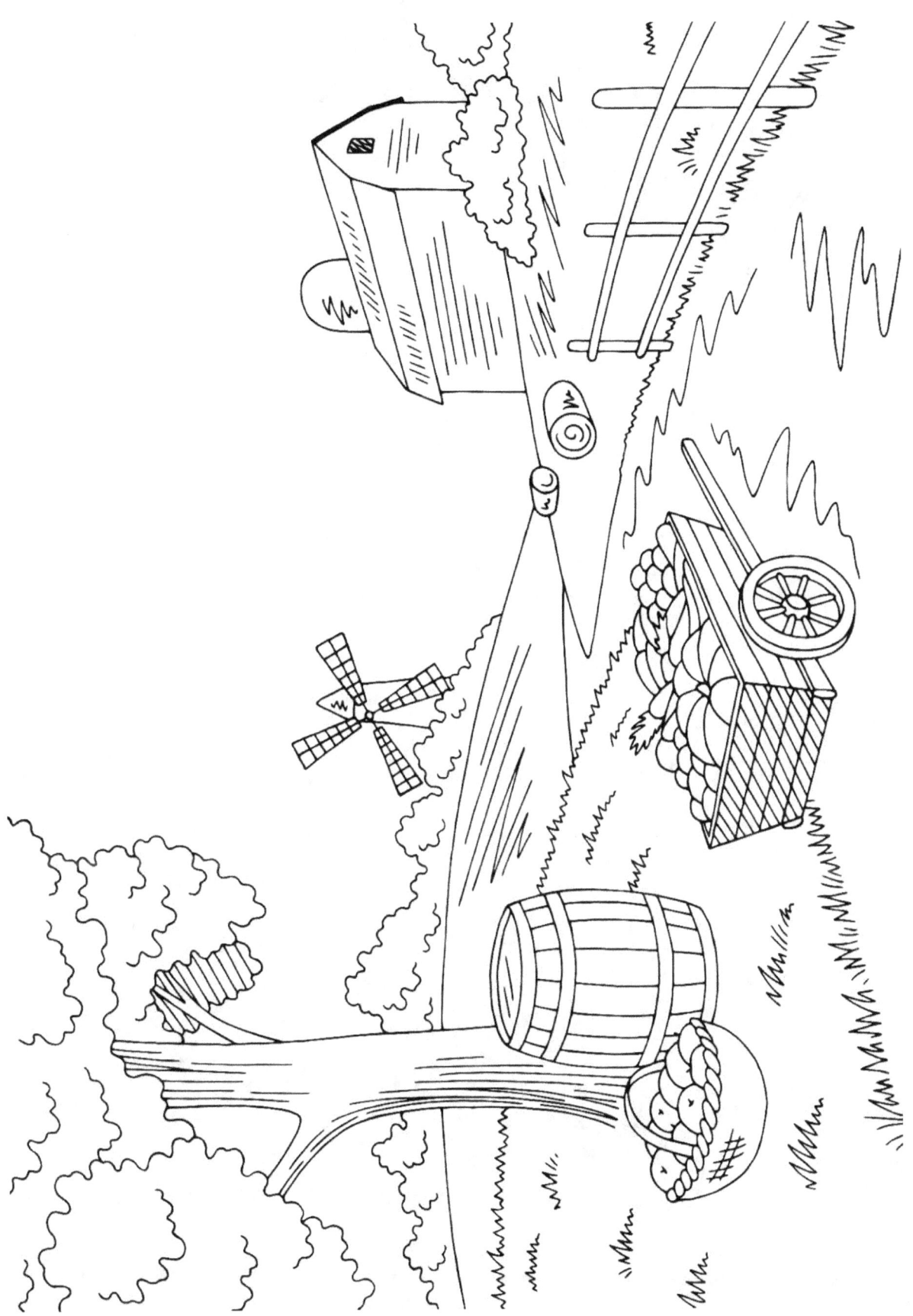

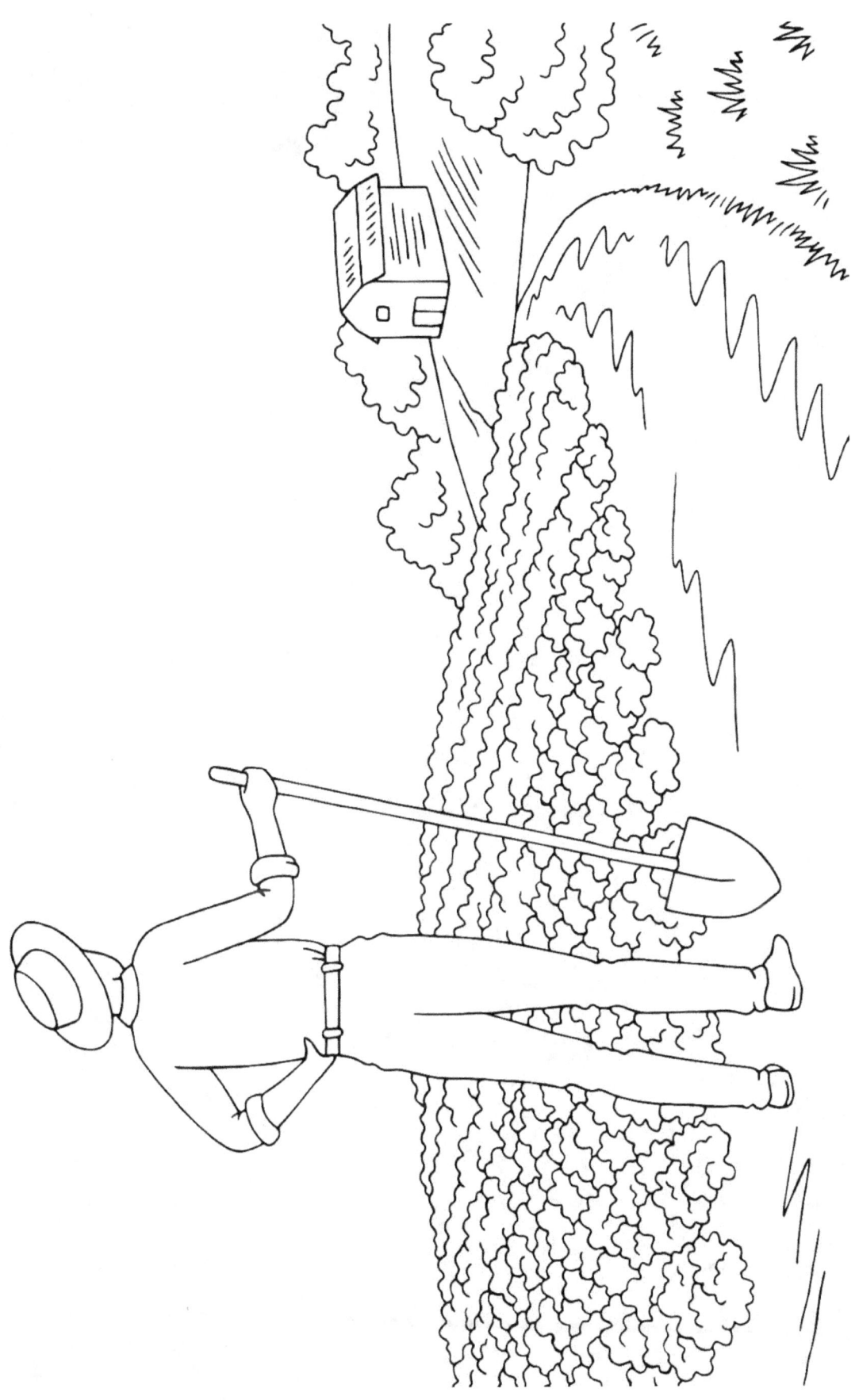

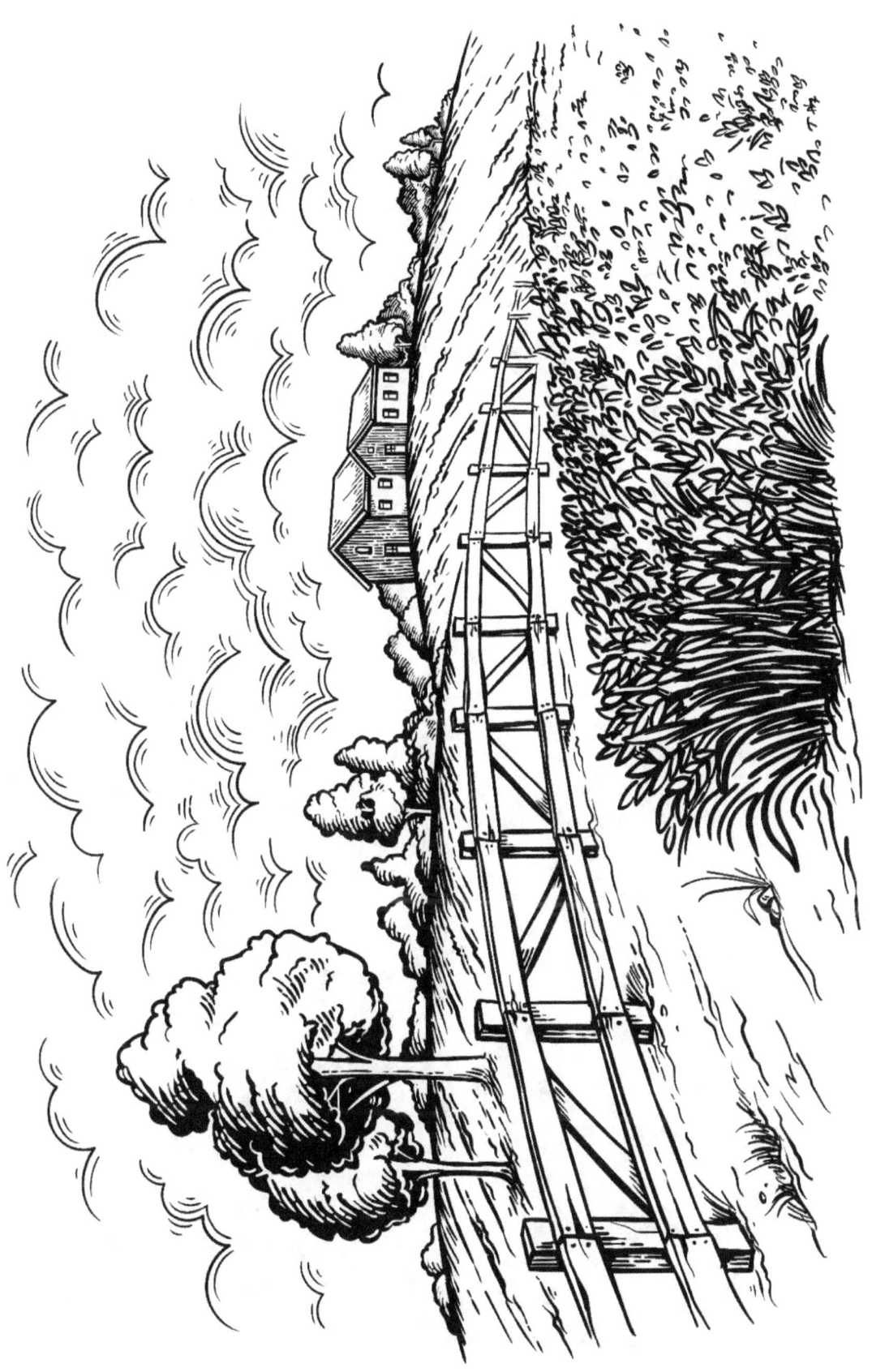

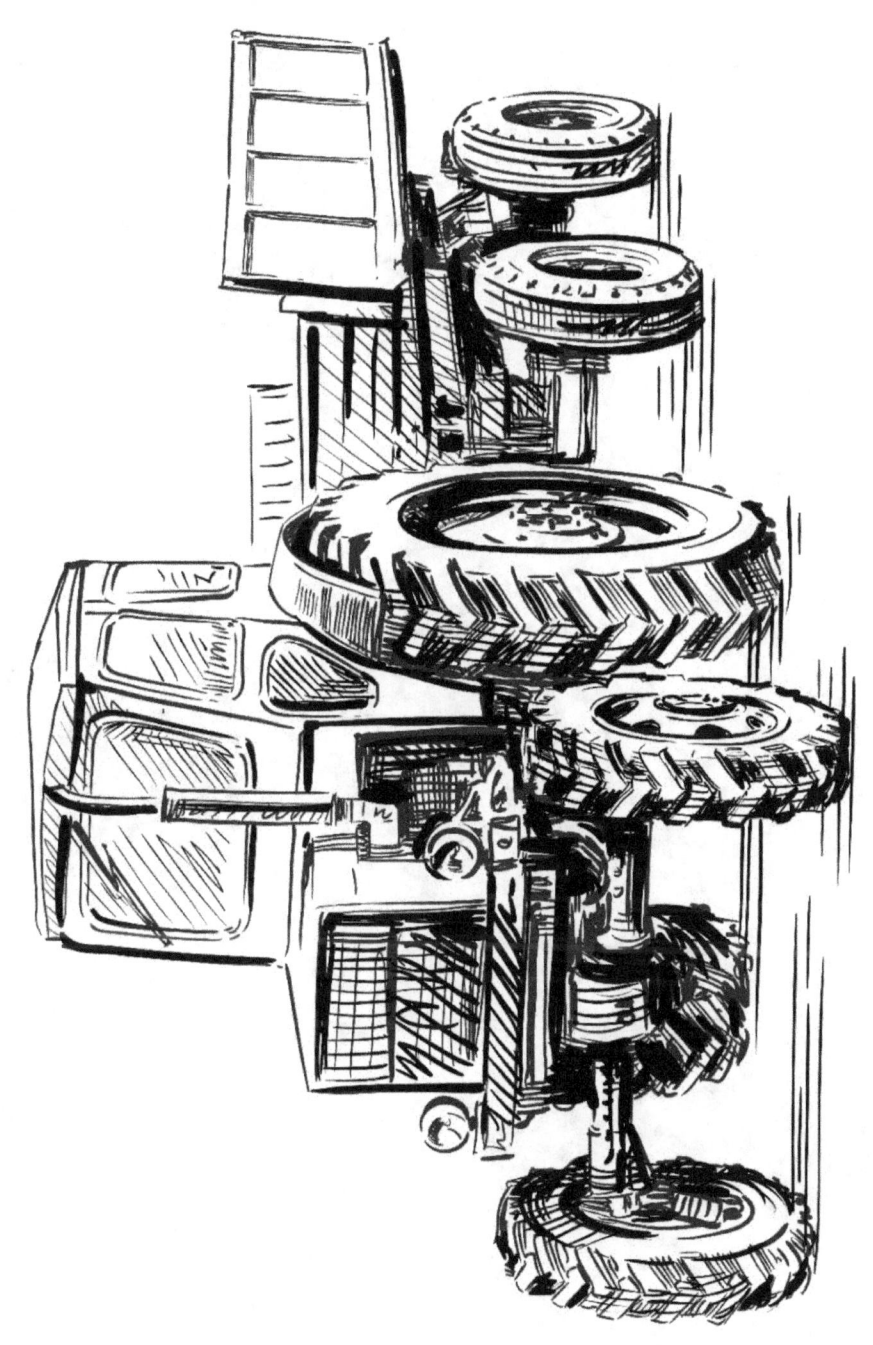

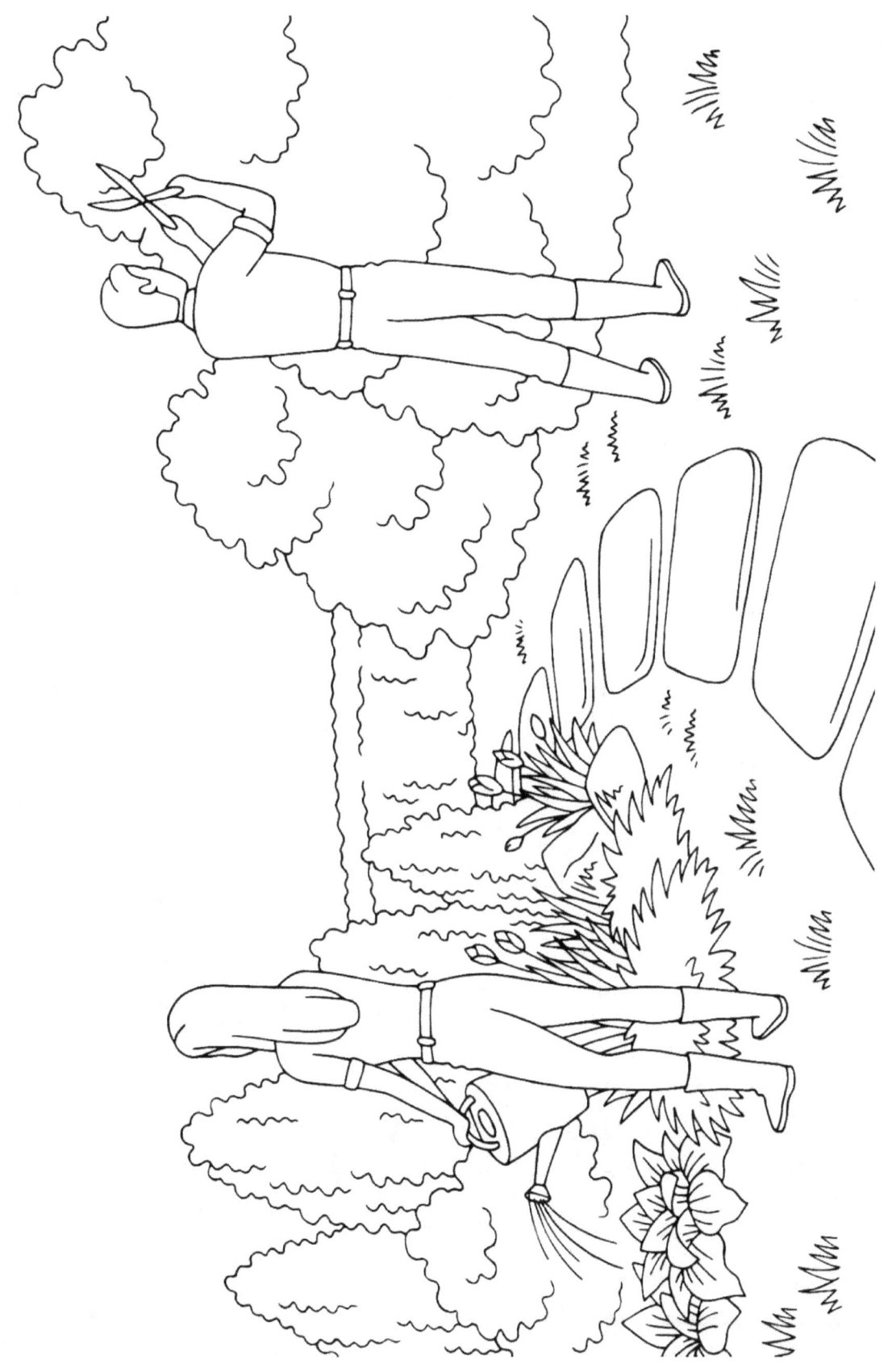

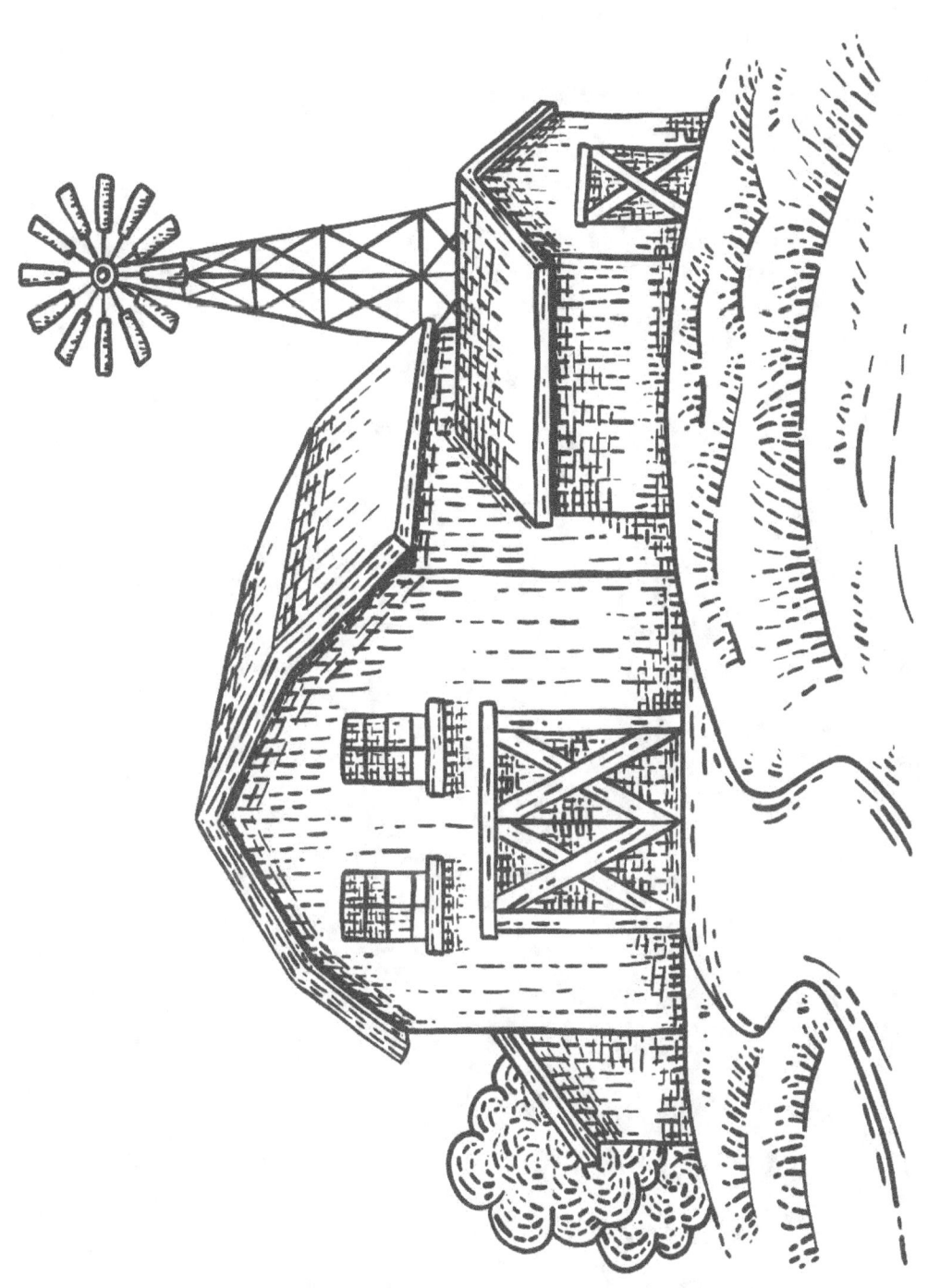

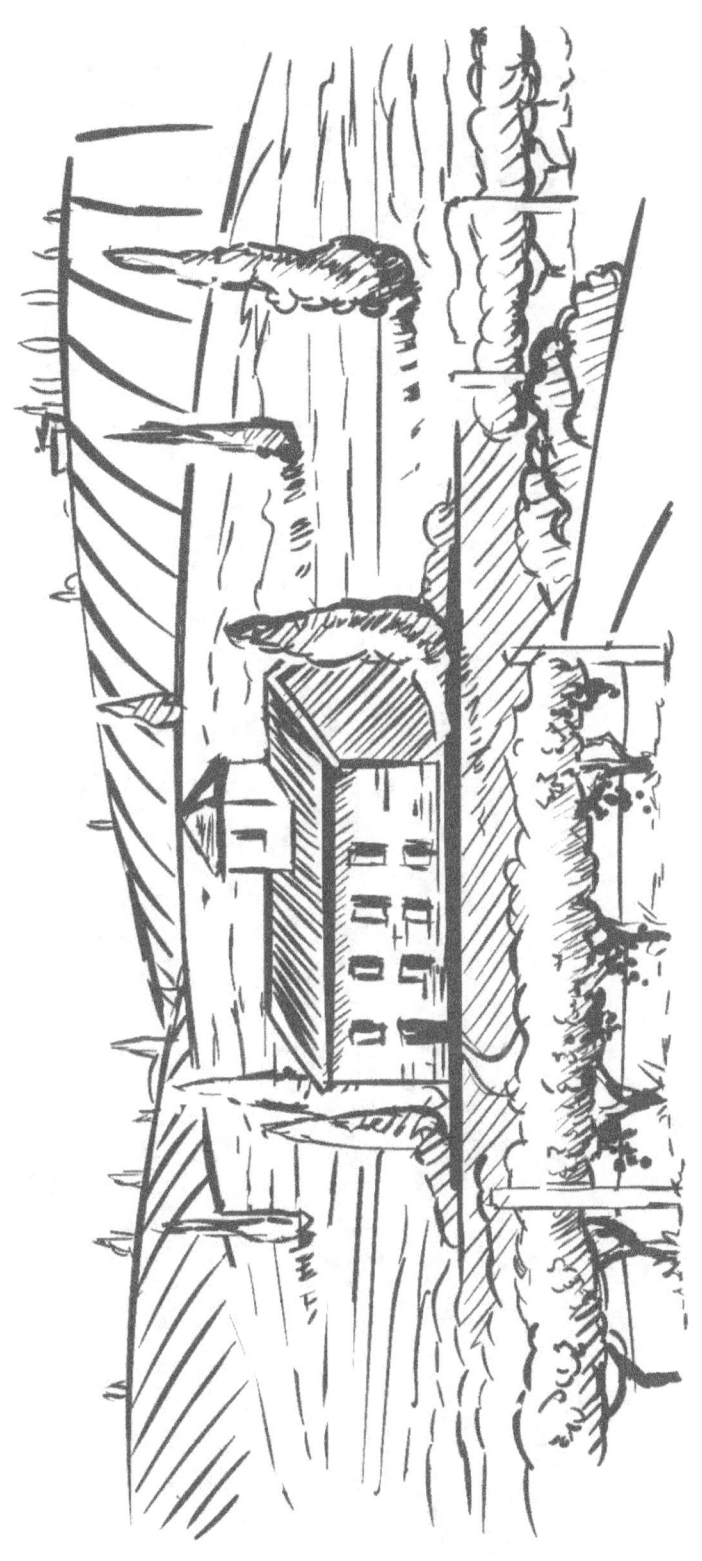

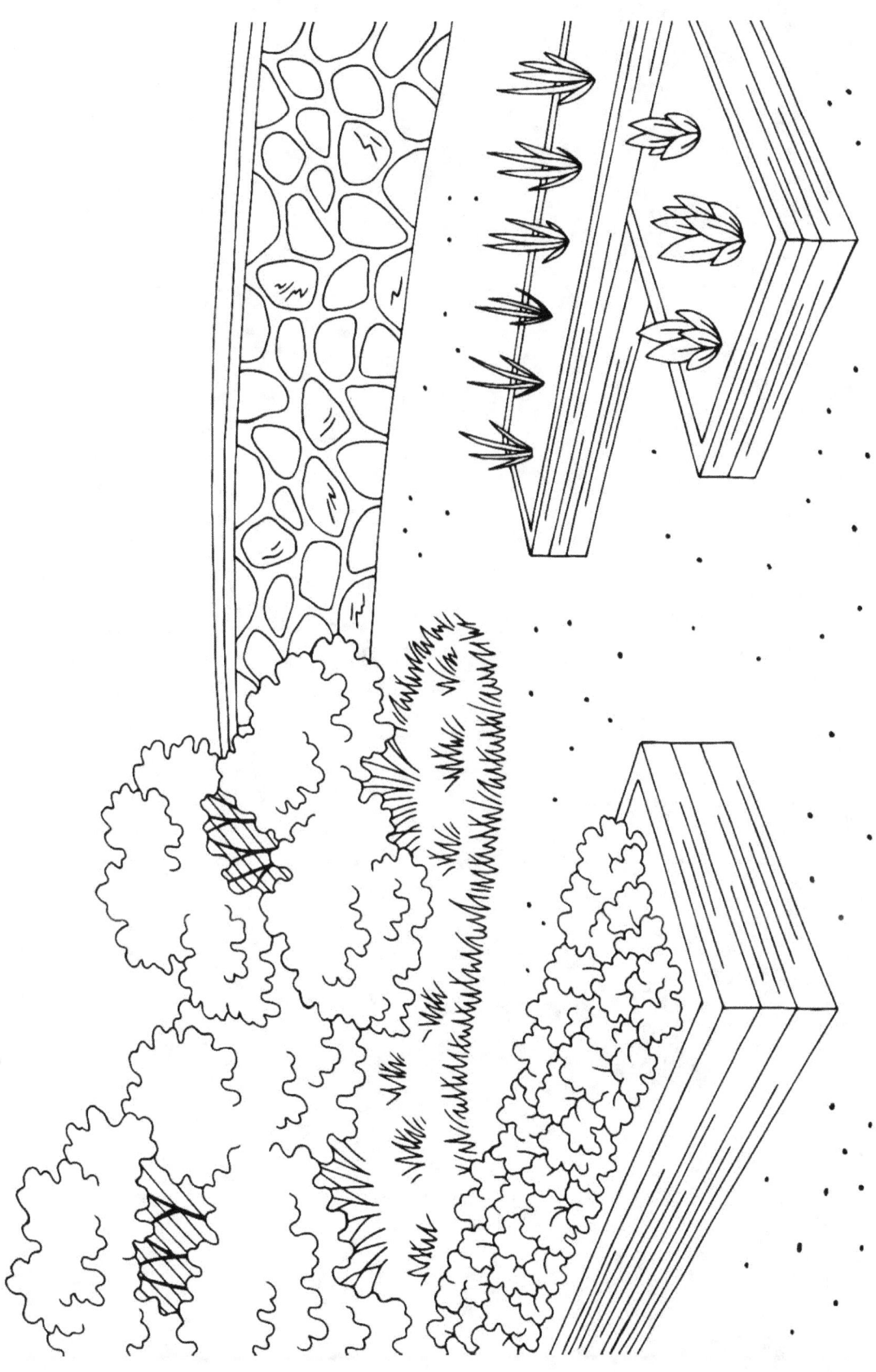

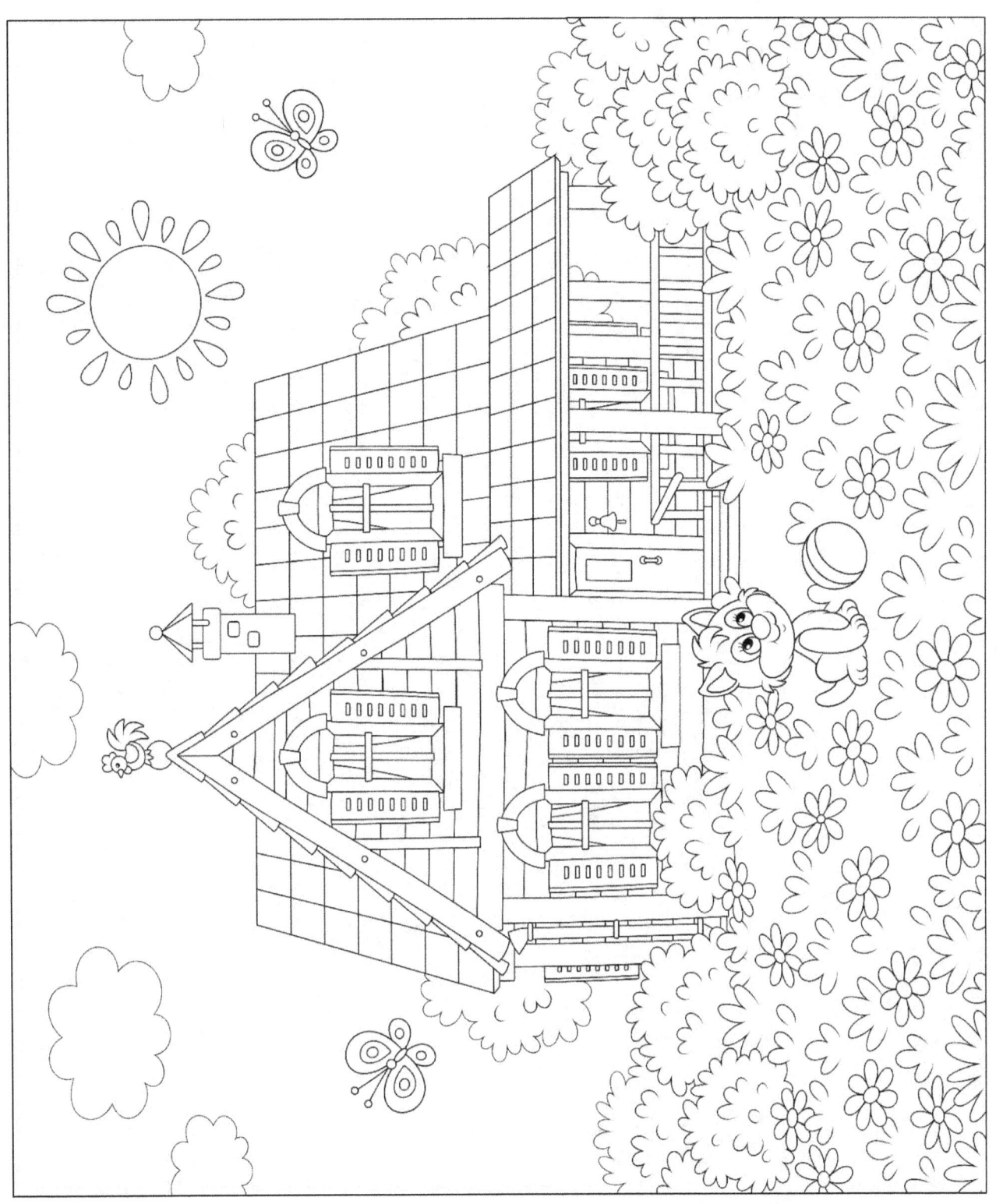

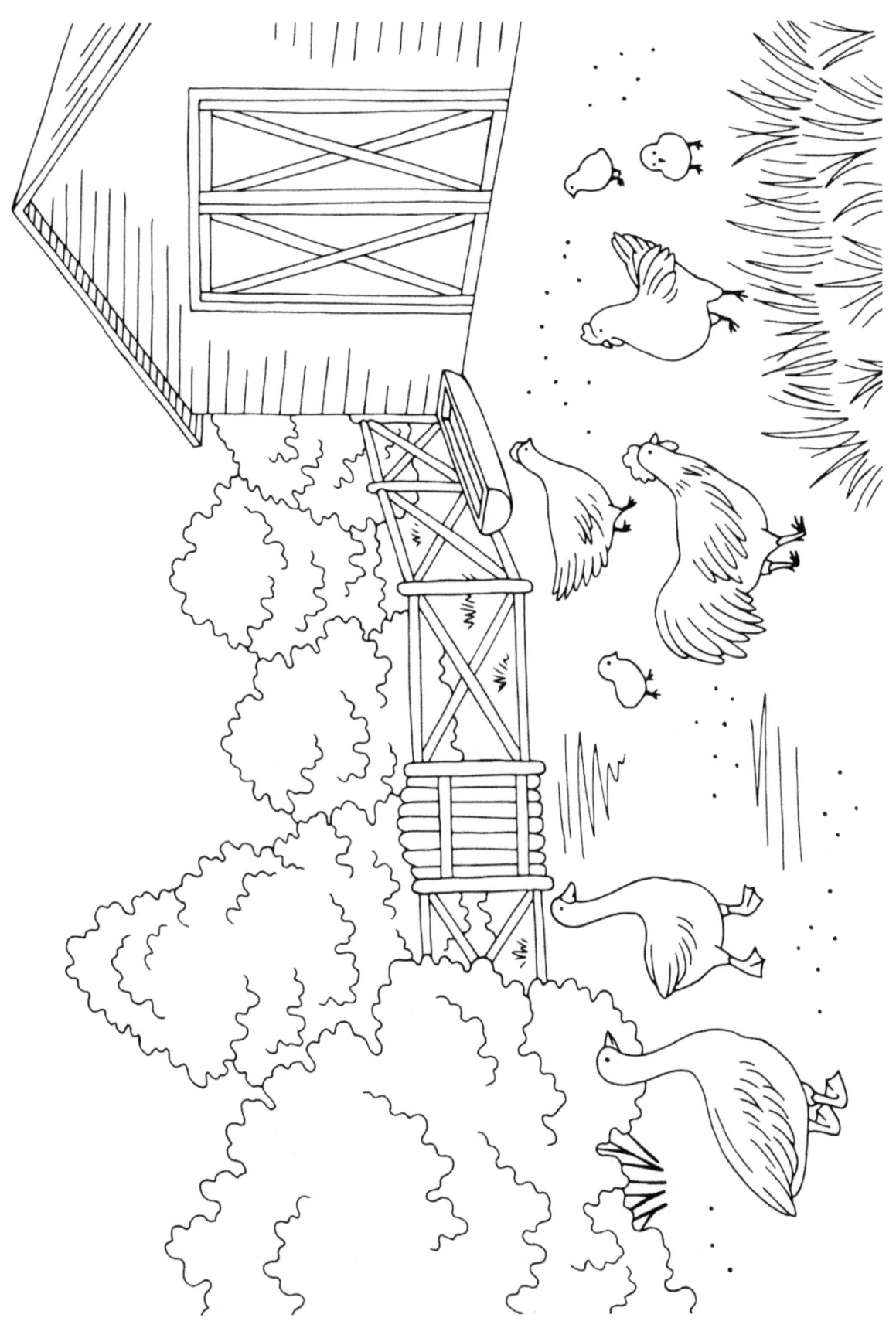

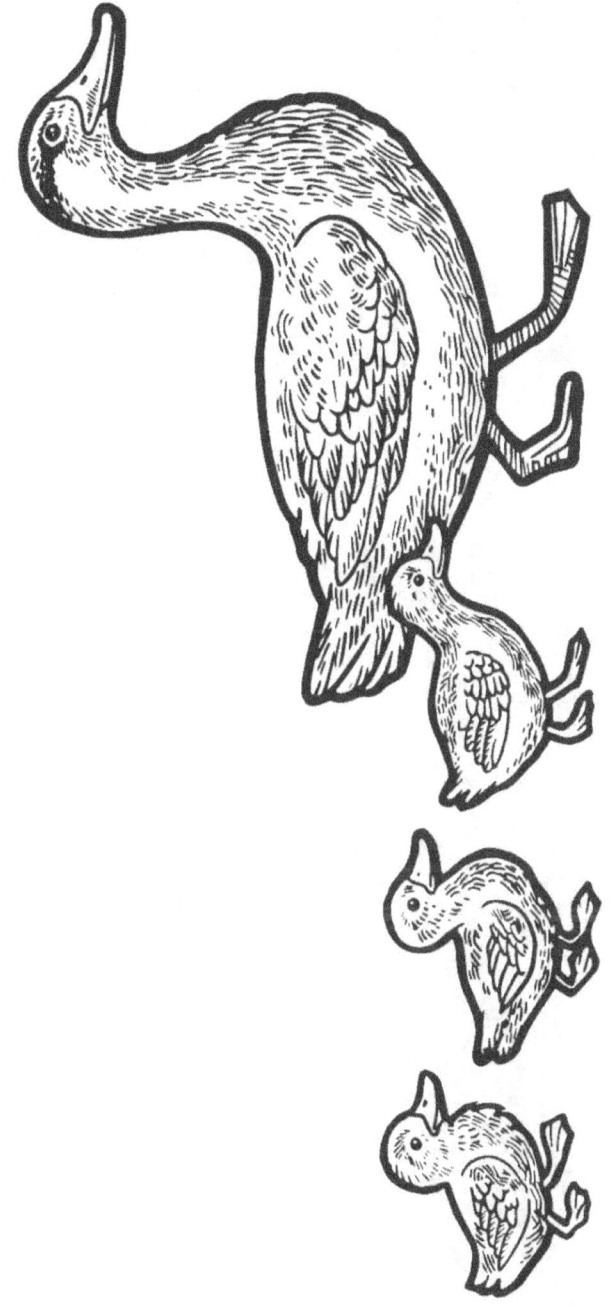

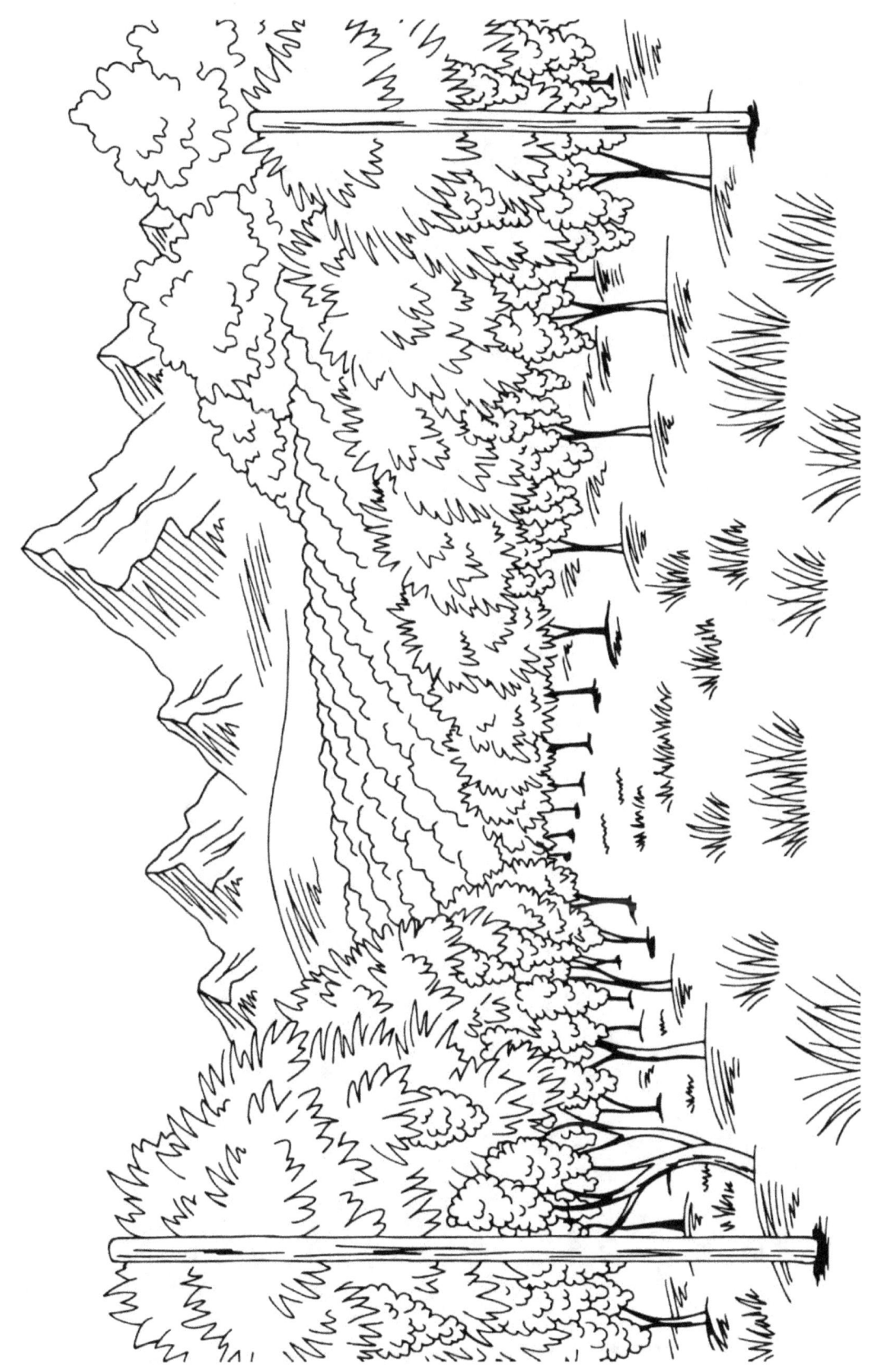

www.ingramcontent.com/pod-product-compliance
Lightning Source LLC
Chambersburg PA
CBHW080557220526
45466CB00010B/3178